Rodney Fuentebella keyframe.

MARVEL STUDIOS
THE INFINITY SAGA

THE ART OF
MARVEL STUDIOS

CAPTAIN AMERICA
CIVIL WAR

WRITTEN BY
JACOB JOHNSTON

FOREWORD BY
ANTHONY & JOE RUSSO

AFTERWORD BY
RYAN MEINERDING

BOOK DESIGN BY
ADAM DEL RE

DUSTJACKET ART BY
RYAN MEINERDING & ANDY PARK

CAPTAIN AMERICA CREATED BY
JOE SIMON & JACK KIRBY

TITAN BOOKS

FOR MARVEL PUBLISHING
JEFF YOUNGQUIST, Editor
SARAH SINGER, Editor, Special Projects
JEREMY WEST, Manager, Licensed Publishing
SVEN LARSEN, VP, Licensed Publishing
DAVID GABRIEL, SVP Print, Sales & Marketing
C.B. CEBULSKI, Editor in Chief

FOR MARVEL STUDIOS 2016
KEVIN FEIGE, President
LOUIS D'ESPOSITO, Co-President
VICTORIA ALONSO, Executive Vice President, Visual Effects
NATE MOORE, Senior Vice President, Production & Development
WILL CORONA PILGRIM, Creative Manager, Research & Development
RYAN POTTER, Principal Counsel
ERIKA DENTON, Clearances Director
RANDY McGOWAN, VP Technical Operations
ELENI ROUSSOS, Digital Asset Coordinator
MITCH BELL, Vice President, Physical Production
ALEXIS AUDITORE, Manager, Physical Assets

MARVEL STUDIOS' THE INFINITY SAGA – CAPTAIN AMERICA: CIVIL WAR: THE ART OF THE MOVIE

ISBN: 9781803368429

10 9 8 7 6 5 4 3 2 1

First edition: April 2025

Published by Titan Books
A division of Titan Publishing Group Ltd
144 Southwark St, London SE1 0UP

www.titanbooks.com

© 2025 MARVEL

No similarity between any of the names, characters, persons, and/or institutions in this book with those of any living or dead person or institution is intended, and any such similarity that may exist is purely coincidental.

Did you enjoy this book? We love to hear from our readers. Please e-mail us at: readerfeedback@titanemail.com or write to Reader Feedback at the above address.

To receive advance information, news, competitions, and exclusive offers online, please sign up for the Titan newsletter on our website: www.titanbooks.com

No part of this publication may be reproduced, stored in a retrieval system, or transmitted, in any form or by any means without the prior written permission of the publisher, nor be otherwise circulated in any form of binding or cover other than that in which it is published and without a similar condition being imposed on the subsequent purchaser.

A CIP catalogue record for this title is available from the British Library.

Printed in China

Rodney Fuentebella keyframe.

Ryan Meinerding keyframe.

CONTENTS

8 FOREWORD
BY ANTHONY & JOE RUSSO

10 INTRODUCTION
THE FALL OF AN EMPIRE

16 CHAPTER ONE
SHOWDOWN IN LAGOS

64 CHAPTER TWO
THE SOKOVIA ACCORDS

80 CHAPTER THREE
CAT AND MOUSE

118 CHAPTER FOUR
MIND GAMES

150 CHAPTER FIVE
CIVIL WAR

204 CHAPTER SIX
ORIGINAL SINS

252 CHAPTER SEVEN
MARKETING CAPTAIN AMERICA: CIVIL WAR

264 AFTERWORD
BY RYAN MEINERDING

266 CONTRIBUTOR BIOS

268 ACKNOWLEDGMENTS

271 ARTIST CREDITS

We've got to be honest: Captain America was never our favorite super hero growing up. While there was certainly something to admire in a fictional character invented to fight Hitler before his country joined the real war, the story of Steve Rogers didn't completely win us over. His strength and toughness were inspiring, but there was something about his unshakable moral certainty, his overwhelming mix of patriotism and propaganda, that left us wanting a little more complexity and a little more edge. For kids like us growing up in the '70s and '80s, the character had fallen out of sync with the times. He was a black-and-white-character in a gray world. To counter that feeling, we would try to imagine him as Steve McQueen in an effort to lend him a coolness that excited us. We were kids looking for a way to love the character.

Of all the good fortune we've had in our careers, nothing tops being invited by Marvel Studios to direct *Captain America: The Winter Soldier*. The movie drew its inspiration from a comic run written by Ed Brubaker, and while that run missed our childhoods, it reinterpreted the character in exactly the way we had been wanting. Now we were being given the opportunity to do in a movie what we had dreamt of as fanboys: texturing and even subverting the patriot through a story that led him to question his country and break orders.

For us, *Captain America: Civil War* is the completion of that subversion. The film moves Steve Rogers past the flaws in his country to finally confront the flaws in himself. This is what makes him a true hero in the classical sense. Despite all the greatness he is capable of, he is flawed, and he is human. And this is a Captain America that we can love.

We couldn't have made this film without the talents and vision of our many collaborators, and we are deeply grateful to them. This book represents some of their work. We hope you enjoy it as we have.

Anthony & Joe Russo

INTRODUCTION
THE FALL OF AN EMPIRE

Since his salvation from the ice at the end of Marvel's *Captain America: The First Avenger*, Steve Rogers has been a man out of time. His convictions, rivaled only by his strategic prowess, are the foundation of what makes Captain America a great hero and the Avengers' fearless leader. As we, the audience, have watched Captain America evolve through the events in the Marvel Cinematic Universe, Cap has watched the world around him change—rapidly. Steve Rogers is no stranger to war. Consequently, he understands the nature of sacrifice, as well as the unwelcome truth of war's casualties. And he understands the inevitability of collateral damage: an alien invasion in *Marvel's The Avengers* that practically leveled New York; a Dark Elf attack in Marvel's *Thor: The Dark World* that almost wiped out the human race; the reveal in Marvel's *Captain America: The Winter Soldier* that Hydra had infiltrated S.H.I.E.L.D. and was planning to kill millions; and finally an entire city lifted into the air—and dropped just after evacuation—in Marvel's *Avengers: Age of Ultron*.

According to Marvel Studios President Kevin Feige, all of these events—along with Steve Rogers and Tony Stark's differing headstrong ideals—are the basis from which Marvel's *Captain America: Civil War* stems. "It's a Captain America film, it's the third film in the Captain America trilogy, but it also is a film that has a very important place amongst all of the other films that we've made, in particular the other Avengers films. By this point, people know Steve Rogers very, very well. People know Tony Stark very, very well. And we felt it was time to see them [in conflict], because we know their personalities so well—we know how they work together, and we know that they have some issues with each other. They're very, very different people. How would they react if they were faced with an issue that they just disagreed about?

"There's an amazing storyline from the comics called *Civil War*, which is one of the best miniseries that Publishing has produced since I've been at Marvel (for 15 years), and in it there is an event that occurs that causes the governments of the world to say, 'We need to have oversight over these heroes now.' In our story that 'oversight' is basically because of the collateral damage caused during all of the action sequences of the other films." While the *Civil War* comic-book series, written by Mark Millar and illustrated by Steve McNiven, revolves around the Superhuman Registration Act, the central conflict in both the film and comics lies in the characters' choices.

At the onset of the film, William Hurt's Thaddeus "Thunderbolt" Ross, last seen in Marvel's *The Incredible Hulk*, returns as secretary of state. He arrives at the Avengers Facility with an ultimatum in the form of the Sokovia Accords: Allow the United Nations to oversee the Avengers' future endeavors—or be arrested for acting as vigilantes. "Tony Stark surprisingly agrees with this, and he thinks if it helps the world sleep better at night, this is something we need to do—and we actually have no choice, because if we don't allow this to occur, we're not going to be able to operate the way we want to, and we won't be able to do the kind of things [we need] to save the world," Feige explains. "Steve Rogers, on the other hand, says, 'Well, I've worked for authority figures before. I remember when the World Security Council sent a nuclear bomb—against Nick Fury's wishes—to New York City that we had to stop. I remember when the organization I signed up with, S.H.I.E.L.D., turned out to in fact be an

The Chitauri invade New York City in *Marvel's The Avengers*.

The Dark Elves wreck London in Marvel's *Thor: The Dark World*.

A S.H.I.E.L.D. Helicarrier crashes into the Triskelion in Washington, D.C., in Marvel's *Captain America: The Winter Soldier*.

The capital city of Sokovia comes under attack in Marvel's *Avengers: Age of Ultron*.

evil organization, Hydra, that I thought I had defeated in World War II. Why do we think it's a good idea to have an authority figure?' There's some people that agree with Steve, and there's some people that agree with Tony, and that becomes the fundamental disagreement between them over the course of the film and ultimately leads to the inherent conflict of the film."

To bring this epic saga to the screen, Joe and Anthony Russo, who directed Marvel's *Captain America: The Winter Soldier*, returned to helm the continuation of Steve Rogers' story. The pair knew Civil War would be a perfect choice to continue crafting a grounded, super-hero thriller while balancing an intricate character story. "The concept of *Civil War* is very important," Joe Russo says. "We felt like we needed to go in a radical direction if we were going to do another Captain America. So we were strongly advocating for the *Civil War* storyline. Once everyone agreed to it, we sat and carefully broke out the arcs of each character, figured out what we wanted the movie to be, and spent probably close to a year in a room with the writers working on the script."

"Captain America is the leader of the Avengers, and part of that job is holding this growing and disparate group of people together," Anthony Russo explains. "It becomes harder and harder as you move forward, and at some point that is going to come to a tipping point—and that is here in this movie. So that is really, I think, the interesting thing of what happens to Steve Rogers here—sort of 'What happens when it all falls apart?'"

"You've never seen this kind of emotional disarray amongst this group of characters," Joe Russo continues. "You've never seen the stakes this high, because they're personal now. The stakes are driving the characters in a way you've never seen on camera, or in the Marvel Cinematic Universe at this point. It leads to a very difficult and uncomfortable place, so it's what sets it apart from any of the other films up to this point. There is both a physical scale and an emotional scale that I think people haven't seen before."

The fulcrum of this emotional scale extends beyond Steve and Tony's disagreement about the Sokovia Accords. The film also finds Bucky Barnes, a.k.a. the Winter Soldier, in the center of the conflict. Although he was brainwashed and forced into performing the unspeakable acts of assassination hinted at in *The Winter Soldier*, Steve continues to pursue Bucky with a hopeful heart. "I think the strength is the personal story of friendship between Steve Rogers and Bucky Barnes," Executive Producer Nate Moore says. "So as much as *Civil War* is the trappings of the film, it's really about Steve

Art from *Civil War #1* by Steve McNiven, Dexter Vines, and Morry Hollowell.

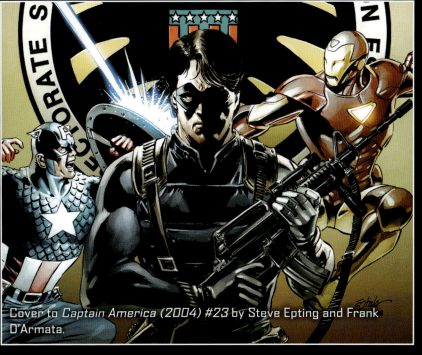

Cover to *Captain America (2004) #23* by Steve Epting and Frank D'Armata.

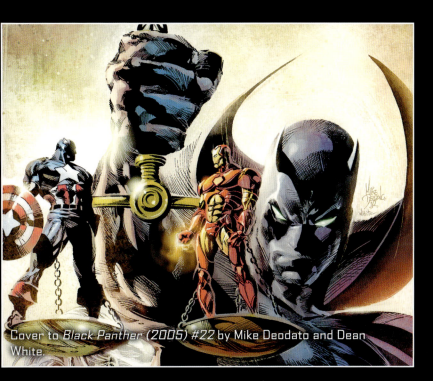

Cover to *Black Panther (2005) #22* by Mike Deodato and Dean White.

making a decision for the first time that's personal over sort of a global version of doing the right thing. Once he does that, once you hook into this idea of Steve Rogers really doing something for himself, it becomes a story that I think, again, is more relatable. And it's that idea of 'How far will you go to rescue your best friend?' Here is Bucky Barnes, who was the Winter Soldier for 80 years—who, in his own way, was a prisoner of war. The idea of choice was taken away from him. The idea of self-determination was taken away from him. And Steve, I think, still sees that glimmer of Bucky Barnes in the Winter Soldier. I think audiences will really plug into this idea of going that extra mile for something you really believe in, and being a beacon of hope and morality so that other characters rally around him."

When Barnes seemingly plants a bomb at the U.N., killing many important officials, Captain America seeks to save him before the government can capture and possibly kill him. Tony leads the charge to apprehend Steve, but he isn't the only one seeking justice. "So much of the *Civil War* story is told from Captain America's point of view. We've brought in Tony Stark to showcase that other side of that argument, and it's really the two of them and the people that team up with them," Feige elaborates. "But at the same time we thought it would be fun to introduce a third side, to introduce a character that audiences have wanted for many, many years, who comes in and is really not agreeing with either side in particular and can represent sort of fresh eyes to see Tony's side of the argument, to see Cap's side of the argument, and frankly to not necessarily care about either side of those arguments because he has his own agenda—and that's T'Challa, the Black Panther."

The Russos were equally eager to introduce Black Panther's unique skill set and complex character traits into the film. "Black Panther brings an intensity that none of the other characters have; there's a real profound energy and edge to the Panther," Joe Russo says. "Chadwick Boseman, who portrays T'Challa in the film, is amazing with conveying that emotion, that energy, through movement and without a lot of words. I think he's carved out a very distinctive character in the Marvel Cinematic Universe. It's not easy coming into the story where the first thing that you're dealing with is tragedy, because it shades the character in a very specific way from the word go. I think Chadwick has done an incredible job of also carving out an arc for himself in a very complicated and crowded movie."

Black Panther isn't the only character making his Marvel Cinematic Universe debut. As Captain America's team grows, Tony Stark begins to explore his options—hopefully finding someone who can bring a non-violent alternative to the table. That person happens to be a 16-year-old kid from Queens: Peter Parker. Stark finds out Parker

Cover to *Civil War* #7 by Steve McNiven, Dexter Vines, and Morry Hollowell.

has created a web-fluid capable of, in Stark's mind, disarming Cap and his team without a real fight. "Something that we at Marvel have been dreaming about for a long time is bringing Spider-Man into the context of the Marvel Cinematic Universe," Moore says. "When we were able to find a deal with Sony, it meant that Spider-Man got to join all of the Avengers in the same way that he has in Publishing for years."

The Russos were specific in how and why Spider-Man would make his inaugural appearance. "We had a very strong point of view of what we wanted to do with the character in this film, and what we felt Marvel and Sony should do with the character moving forward," Joe Russo says. "We were very aggressive on the casting front, looking for the right actor, the right age. I felt it was better to go much younger and to not have somebody who was 30 years old playing a 16-year-old. It was more important to find somebody more age-appropriate who would convey that energy—that naivete that would come from being that age and having that kind of power. We also thought it was really interesting to take that naivete and smash it into the cynicism of Tony Stark. What better way to bring that character into the MCU than through Tony Stark?"

With all of these characters intricately maneuvering through a complex and compelling story, the question remains: Who is the real villain? Past films have clearly defined the villain's motivations and intentions. However, the Russos were determined to make a film in which everyone was a "little bit right and a little bit wrong," Joe Russo says.

"The story of *Civil War* is primarily about the conflict between Captain America and Iron Man, and between the sides that agree with each of them based on this mandate that is coming down from the governments of the world," Feige says. "At the same time, we are introducing another villain; there is somebody who is operating in the shadows, and while not responsible for the events that lead up to *Civil War*, is fanning the flames and is utilizing the conflict to his own advantage. That's something that is going to have a very unique element not unlike the thriller elements of *Captain America: The Winter Soldier* that carries through into *Civil War*, and it does give a very different dynamic to the heroes who at a certain point are realizing, 'We're fighting each other, but there's something else happening here; somebody is using the fact that we're fighting each other to their advantage.' He's a very different kind of villain. We wanted to see what it would it be like for a villain to take on the Avengers without throwing a single punch. We've cast Daniel Brühl to play this role—he is so cunning, and he's such a great actor who has this presence that, even without an army and without an armored suit and without a skilled fighting style, he comes very, very close to undoing them forever."

While keeping the film grounded and realistic, the Russo brothers were adamant about capturing the essence of its comic

Iron Man/Captain America: Casualties of War, Cover A by Jim Cheung, John Dell, and Justin Ponsor.

book counterpart. "Making this film was a completely surreal experience," Joe Russo says. "Having grown up on comics, it's a fantasy of everyone who reads them to see 'Who's stronger than who?' and 'What would happen if your favorite heroes fought each other?' To be out there watching everyone in these costumes running at each other and just thinking, 'Wow, it's the journey from being 10 years old on the back porch of my buddy's house reading *Secret Wars* to this?' It's amazing to see how much impact this mythology has on the people you grew up with, because they ascribe very specific feelings and ideas and emotions to those characters. They represent something very important to people. To put them in conflict with one another, to have all those characters—to have Panther standing next to Spider-Man standing next to Iron Man and War Machine, then we pan over to see Captain America with Ant-Man and Scarlet Witch and Falcon—it was emotional."

"Part of the fun of telling these kinds of stories on a massive scale is being able to set up storylines that you may not be able to see coming two or three movies down the line," Moore adds. "When you're talking about an event this big in *Civil War*, one that literally splits the Avengers apart, it can only have repercussions for what's to come."

Iron Man/Captain America: Casualties of War, Cover B by Jim Cheung, John Dell, and Justin Ponsor.

Cover to *Civil War #3* by Steve McNiven, Dexter Vines, and Morry Hollowell.

CHAPTER ONE
SHOWDOWN IN LAGOS

The Avengers have changed since we last saw them. They've lost comrades-in-arms and gained new allies—and with a new team comes a new direction. At the onset of the film, we find Captain America leading a reconnaissance mission in Lagos, the largest city in Nigeria. "The opening set piece reintroduces audiences to the characters of Steve Rogers, Sam Wilson, and Natasha Romanoff as a trio," Executive Producer Nate Moore says. "We kind of see them as the cornerstone of the Captain America franchise. At the same time, it folds in a new character: Wanda Maximoff, the Scarlet Witch. To see that dynamic—this sort of new team forming as they're trying to hunt down Crossbones in Nigeria in a completely new setting—is really special."

Production Designer Owen Paterson and Directors Joe and Anthony Russo approached the world of Marvel's *Captain America: Civil War* with a grounded, real-world eye. "Joe and Anthony, I think they're both really good storytellers. They wanted to achieve a realistic nature to the film. They didn't want it to be overly stylized," Paterson explains. "They wanted it to feel like we were in real places, hence why we chose the locations we did. Though it's a great-looking, visually dynamic space, it's also very real, and it's connected to outside spaces. They didn't want it overly flashy. They wanted to tell their story, and keep the focus about the characters and their exchanges." That storytelling drive is at the center of the collaborative process for conceptualizing, altering, and creating these environments and characters—and as with previous installments in the Marvel Cinematic Universe, it begins with the artists.

Rodney Fuentebella concept art.

STEVE ROGERS / CAPTAIN AMERICA

Head of Visual Development Ryan Meinerding has designed Captain America since the hero's initial appearance in Marvel's *Captain America: The First Avenger*. According to Meinerding, the evolution of Steve Rogers' look is based on both the preference of the director and the nature of the story. "The Russo brothers have very specific taste in costumes, and usually that involves tactical and realistic design elements," Meinerding says. "The suit in *Civil War* is a simplified version of the *Avengers: Age of Ultron* costume. The Russos thought the costume was successful, but felt there were some design flourishes, like the white on the arms and the red detailing around the chest, that wouldn't necessarily be realistic in the more grounded film they wanted to make."

Ryan Meinerding concept art.

CHAPTER ONE: SHOWDOWN IN LAGOS

During an exploratory phase, Meinerding adapted Captain America's iconic chain mail from the comic books into a practical design. "I'm a huge fan of Cap's traditional scale armor, and I've always wanted to make it work," he explains. "When Tony Stark conceptually started being the one designing and building the Avengers' costumes, that costume felt a little more possible in the worlds we were making. Practically, it's a challenge to accomplish without feeling like it's something you've seen before. This was an attempt in doing that kind of armor, but in a more tactical and modern way. I focused on creating pointy U-shapes with more hard-edged angles to make it feel a bit more tough and read as bulletproof instead of just shiny scales. The other design part of it is that each one of the scales are designed to fit around the star, which is the classic look. The star is simply cut into the U-shape—I was trying to design something that sort of fits together perfectly instead of cutting a shape out of a bunch of U-shaped scales."

Ryan Meinerding concept art.

In early plans for the Lagos opening, Captain America wasn't intended to sport his red-white-and-blue look. Meinerding's initial design passes sought to balance that costume's super-hero elements with a more subtle approach to the overall aesthetic. "These designs were meant to be an in-between of Cap's Avengers look and a more casual, plain-clothes look. The idea was he could put on a bulletproof vest and go into action without having to walk through the streets in full costume."

Ryan Meinerding concept art.

Ryan Meinerding concept art.

CHAPTER ONE: SHOWDOWN IN LAGOS

SAM WILSON / FALCON

Audiences first glimpsed Sam Wilson's new costume in Marvel's *Ant-Man* during a brief scuffle with the film's titular hero. Falcon's design has undergone a subtle evolution from his first cinematic appearance, yet it remains grounded in realism. "The fundamental elements of his original design carried over—such as the goggles, collapsible wings, backpack with thrusters, and gauntlets," Concept Artist Josh Nizzi says. "After exploring a number of alternative ideas, we decided to leave the design of the wings virtually unchanged aside from some additional coloring, bringing in more of his iconic red color. I'd say the new Falcon design feels like he shops at the same stores as Captain America and the Winter Soldier. I'm hoping they have a shopping sequence in one of these movies."

Josh Nizzi concept art.

When we met Falcon in Marvel's *Captain America: The Winter Soldier*, his gear was enhanced military tech. Visual Effects Supervisor Dan Deleeuw notes that after "earning his wings" in that film, "Falcon has evolved from being a brave guy to a real super hero." And a new status meant a new look. "Falcon's military tech has been replaced with Stark tech," Deleeuw explains. "This means a more refined, smaller backpack and a variation on the carbon-fiber wings we used in the previous film. We've added additional articulation points to the wings so he can pull them in front of him to function along the lines of a Middle Ages long shield: this allows him to deflect bullets."

Josh Nizzi concept art.

CHAPTER ONE: SHOWDOWN IN LAGOS

REDWING DRONE

In addition to Falcon's new look, he's acquired a pseudo sidekick: a red birdlike drone called Redwing. In the comics, Redwing is an actual bird that serves as Sam Wilson's ally and eye-in-the-sky. For the Marvel Cinematic Universe, the filmmakers focused on augmenting Falcon's arsenal by integrating today's technology. "The idea was to give Falcon additional tools to assist in being a watchman in the sky. The hard part is when you're always so high up, you can't always see what's happening down on the ground," Executive Producer and Head of Physical Production Victoria Alonso says. "This was a way for us to get an additional set of eyes on the ground while keeping Falcon surveying up high. We're also very much in the era of drones—I think it's in the lingo of today's society of what drones can do for you."

"I'm really happy with the Redwing design and the integration into the backpack," Nizzi says. "Redwing has enough birdlike qualities to reference the comic and have some personality, but is military enough to not be silly. Cutting-edge military drones have a pretty similar profile to diving falcons, so that was a pretty obvious place to start. We tried to find the right balance to convey the bird idea but still make it appear like plausible technology, and hopefully something iconic people would remember."

MISSILE LAUNCHER DOOR OPEN

CLOSED

CLOSED

"There are some levels of autonomy to the drone," Dan Deleeuw adds. "It can kind of fly on its own. It's not quite its own character yet…but maybe one day."

Josh Nizzi concept art.

CHAPTER ONE: SHOWDOWN IN LAGOS

NATASHA ROMANOFF / BLACK WIDOW

Since her debut in Marvel's *Iron Man 2*, Black Widow's appearance has remained fairly consistent. Each subsequent version has featured an upgrade—a new color breakup or various design changes—but as Lead Visual Development Concept Illustrator Andy Park points out, the simplicity of her look makes the Avengers a little more relatable. "Black Widow and Hawkeye have the most grounded looks, being the special agents they are," Park says. "They are both still heroes that are 'super,' but their humanness helps ground the team to an even more relatable place than the ones who are 'beyond human' can."

Andy Park concept art.

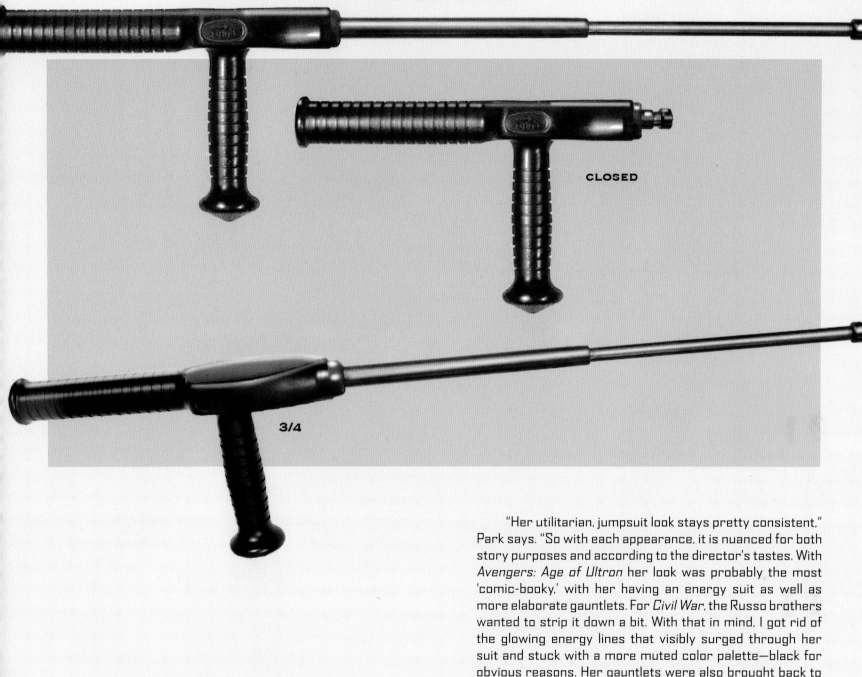

OPEN AND EXTENDED

CLOSED

3/4

CHAPTER ONE: SHOWDOWN IN LAGOS

"Her utilitarian, jumpsuit look stays pretty consistent," Park says. "So with each appearance, it is nuanced for both story purposes and according to the director's tastes. With *Avengers: Age of Ultron* her look was probably the most 'comic-booky,' with her having an energy suit as well as more elaborate gauntlets. For *Civil War*, the Russo brothers wanted to strip it down a bit. With that in mind, I got rid of the glowing energy lines that visibly surged through her suit and stuck with a more muted color palette—black for obvious reasons. Her gauntlets were also brought back to the simpler yet classic cylinder bracelet. Everything ends up being more streamlined and simple."

John Eaves concept art.

27

"Natasha's look in the opening was all about finding a blend of undercover tourist while still being chic," Costume Designer Judianna Makovsky says. "Due to the tropical climate of Lagos, we wanted to keep her away from anything too dark, especially black. We landed on this more earth-toned jacket that was also very action-friendly. So often in these movies it's easy to settle on a design that's visually intriguing, but then it becomes about how to make it action-friendly. The stunts these characters are doing are oftentimes extremely involved, and we need the clothes to move with them, not against them."

Christian Cordella concept art.

Christian Cordella concept art.

CHAPTER ONE: SHOWDOWN IN LAGOS

WANDA MAXIMOFF / SCARLET WITCH

At the end of Marvel's *Avengers: Age of Ultron*, Wanda Maximoff—a.k.a the Scarlet Witch—reveals her stylized hero costume as she floats down to join her teammates in their new training facility. "It was a lot more 'costumey' than her basic Sokovian look throughout the film, which was essentially just her civilian clothing," Andy Park says. "So with *Civil War*, the Russo brothers wanted to tone down her new look to a more grounded version.

"I always try to juggle the need to design a character according to the requirements necessary to the story as well as the director, while trying to respect the source material. Scarlet Witch in the comic book has a pretty evocative costume, and we knew we couldn't go that far. But I did do a version that had her wearing a type of headband as a nod to the classic headdress she dons in the comic books."

Andy Park concept art.

CHAPTER ONE: SHOWDOWN IN LAGOS

Park's design was the first step in the journey from concept to film. "Designing costumes for these larger-than-life characters is a very collaborative process between many players in the production," he explains. "But the main collaboration happens between our Visual Development Department and the costume designer, in this case Judianna Makovsky. Through the process of approval, production, and creation of these costumes, the look can evolve and grow in many ways. At times, the end result is a very one-to-one translation of the original concept-design illustration, and at other times it will evolve and change depending on so many factors. In Scarlet Witch's case, the design started with my concept illustration, and during the actual creation of the costume by Judianna's team, it evolved to what you see in the film. It's pretty amazing watching a costume brought to life by amazing costume designers like Judianna."

Andy Park concept art.

As one of the team's newest members, Scarlet Witch is still coming into her powers while also learning what it takes to be an Avenger. "She has an extensive power set that she isn't quite certain how to use," Victoria Alonso says. "We're following her on this journey of trying to figure out how to be a team player, how her powers integrate within the group. We're focusing on sculpting her as a character who grows from the repercussions of her actions and does not allow them to cloud her judgment of what is right."

Christian Cordella concept art.

CHAPTER ONE: SHOWDOWN IN LAGOS

Judianna Makovsky used Park's concept to tailor Wanda's costume, eventually arriving at the character's on-screen appearance. "The Russo brothers wanted to strip away some of the more 'super hero' elements of her look. She isn't that person yet," Makovsky says. "We put her in more real clothes with a fairly simple coat and pants. The jacket also opens in the back to create a really nice sense of movement when she's flying or when she's fighting."

Christian Cordella concept art.

BROCK RUMLOW / CROSSBONES

Much like that of his comic-book counterpart, S.H.I.E.L.D.-turned-Hydra Agent Brock Rumlow's cinematic look was intended to instill fear, while simultaneously mirroring his personality. "As with any character I've worked on before in the Marvel Cinematic Universe, I started by researching how he is portrayed in the comic books," Concept Artist Rodney Fuentebella says. "Crossbones is a relentless, cold-blooded mercenary who's a bit off his rocker. To me, the iconic 'X' across his chest and the skull-painted face mask were both important comic-book cues that defined Crossbones visually. To keep the character grounded, I first tried integrating straps and other items from his uniform to create the silhouette. Eventually, a more haphazardly painted approach with white ended up working much better for this character, and also showed a bit of his crazed personality."

Rodney Fuentebella concept art.

CHAPTER ONE: SHOWDOWN IN LAGOS

After portraying Rumlow in Marvel's *Captain America: The Winter Soldier*, actor Frank Grillo embraced the return of the nihilistic mercenary with a "sense of mayhem." "I love villains, and I thought this would be a great opportunity to have just an unapologetic, murderous, venomous villain who could kind of stand his ground with these super heroes."

The final costume's appearance mirrored Fuentebella's concept, and brought the character to life in a visceral and grounded way. "To me, the look of it was kind of post-apocalyptic," Grillo says. "It wasn't clean, and it looked like he had put it together himself from whatever he had laying around. It suits the character. When I get in the suit, I feel mean—I feel angry."

Rodney Fuentebella concept art.

Likewise, Judianna Makovsky and her team fabricated the Crossbones costume by repurposing everyday materials. "We started with real body armor and adjusted it to mirror his maniacal personality—something that feels dangerous and still a bit clunky," she says. "Crossbones isn't a high-tech, magical scientist—he's not going to whip up an outfit that feels unreasonably complex. The 'X' across his chest was actually one of the most challenging things to get right. We wanted it to feel crudely applied, and not like it was overly 'designed.' It was a really fulfilling moment when we figured out how to make it work."

Rodney Fuentebella concept art.

Rodney Fuentebella concept art.

CHAPTER ONE: SHOWDOWN IN LAGOS

Rodney Fuentebella concept art.

SCPS Unlimited concept art.

Rodney Fuentebella concept art.

Rounding out Crossbones' arsenal are two crudely fabricated, but extremely dangerous, gauntlets. "The idea of the gauntlets was to give Crossbones a weapon against Captain America that further accentuates his demented and ruthless nature," Fuentebella says. "The Russo brothers wanted the gauntlets to feel as if he'd gotten the parts from a hardware store and made them at home or a shop—he's no Tony Stark. The gauntlets had to feel authentic in a practical manner—more specifically, something that a person of limited technical capacity and also a little crazy could create. They had to look like they were made in his garage or workshop with sloppy welds and makeshift straps. The gauntlets also gave Crossbones' silhouette a stronger, more unique, and somewhat sinister feel."

Rodney Fuentebella concept art.

"I did a lot of research on construction equipment like jackhammers and other pneumatic tools," Fuentebella says. "The goal was to also land on something that didn't feel too heavy or inaccessible—otherwise he'd be bogged down and wouldn't actually be able to land a hit. It went through many iterations before finally landing on something that worked both conceptually and practically."

Rodney Fuentebella concept art.

CHAPTER ONE: SHOWDOWN IN LAGOS

41

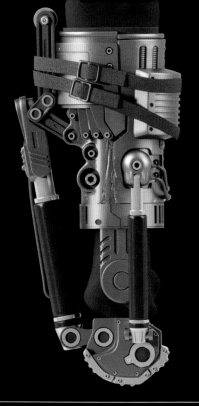
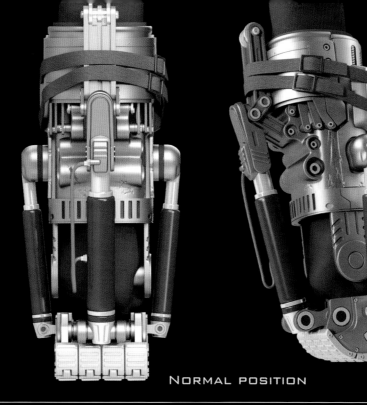

NORMAL POSITION

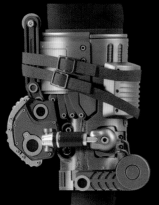
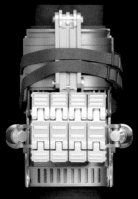

RETRACTED POSITION

Video production company SCPS Unlimited was tasked with the gauntlets' fabrication, and a back-and-forth pipeline was established with the Visual Development team to ensure the design's integrity. "The work that SCPS did was incredible," Fuentebella says. "They realized the concept and made it feel believable. I did some paintovers to give the gauntlets a makeshift feel and added some discoloration, mismatched wires, and some leftover tape with numbers. I wanted the gauntlets to feel like a prototype he is constantly tweaking, adding whatever wires and pieces he has in his shop at the time, and writing notes to himself to indicate what part goes where."

SCPS Unlimited concept art.

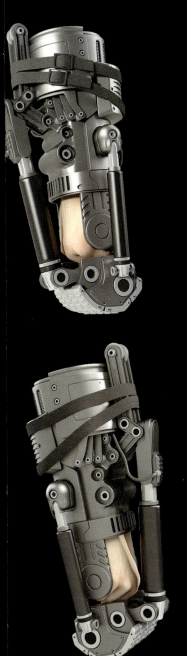

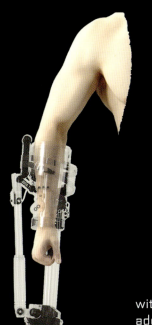

"It is important for me when designing to come up with the stories of how these things get made," Fuentebella adds. "Even if the audience only sees the designs for a short time, creating a backstory of how these gauntlets got made is important for the design process."

extended 4.5"

RUMLOW'S MERCENARIES

Mariano Diaz concept art.

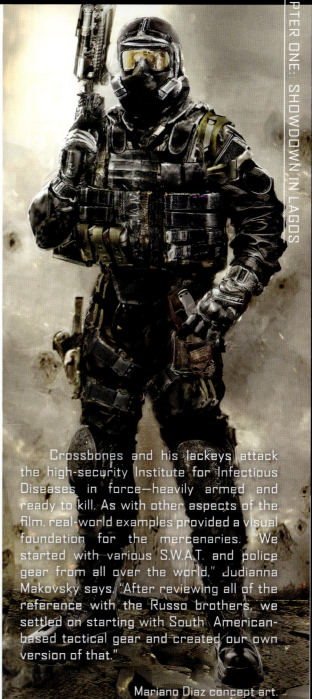

Crossbones and his lackeys attack the high-security Institute for Infectious Diseases in force—heavily armed and ready to kill. As with other aspects of the film, real-world examples provided a visual foundation for the mercenaries. "We started with various S.W.A.T. and police gear from all over the world," Judianna Makovsky says. "After reviewing all of the reference with the Russo brothers, we settled on starting with South American-based tactical gear and created our own version of that."

Mariano Diaz concept art.

INSTITUTE FOR INFECTIOUS DISEASES

As the Avengers rush to stop Crossbones in Lagos, they find themselves at the Institute for Infectious Diseases. Much like the *Lemurian Star* takedown seen at the start of Marvel's *Captain America: The Winter Soldier*, the Russo brothers sought to open *Civil War* with a plausible, high-stakes set piece. "One of the things we were talking about in building the opening of the film was making Crossbones a terrifying figure," Nate Moore says. "Part and parcel to that is giving him an agenda that was both real-world and really, really scary. The Russo brothers never like things to just be linear, so our goal was to sort of suggest he'd been robbing police stations for weapons—but then we find out he's been doing something much worse. What's worse than guns and grenades? Biological weaponry."

While the Institute for Infectious Diseases is a fictional location, the filmmakers had a distinct agenda for choosing its geographical location in Nigeria. "We knew we wanted to introduce the idea of Wakanda and the Black Panther into the narrative," Moore explains. "Therefore it made sense to set it in an African country where there could be Wakandans. It's harder to tell that same story if you're in, say, Amsterdam, and Crossbones robs something terrible and accidentally kills Wakandans there—that feels a little more like a stretch than a neighboring country. It was always an alchemy of 'what's the right opening for the film,' 'what's going to set up Crossbones as a big threat that *has* to be stopped,' and 'how do we organically include Wakandans in the devastation that takes place.'"

Manuel Plank-Jorge keyframe.

Despite the film's global scope, the majority of the scenes were shot in Atlanta. The challenge of physically replicating Nigeria in the American South wwas left to Owen Paterson and his team. "For a moment, we were going to shoot in Puerto Rico to double Lagos—climate-wise, they're very similar, and the shape of the cities are fairly similar, as they both have water elements in the body of the city," Paterson says. Ultimately we went to Atlanta, so we shifted gears.

"The Atlanta Civic Center turned out to be a really good location for us. Tonally, it felt like it lived in the world of Lagos, at least the Lagos that we had researched. The Civic Center isn't a huge hub of activity in Atlanta, so we were able to go in and dress the elements that didn't feel enough like Lagos—for instance, putting in planters with vegetation that is appropriate to the region of Lagos versus what's in Atlanta. We could then take the existing structure and build on it practically and through visual effects to make it look as authentic as possible."

Manuel Plank-Jorge keyframe.

"We took the initial art from the Art Department, as well as the research they had done on how they'd dress the Atlanta locations to double as Africa, and combined it with our own research," Visual Effects Producer Jen Underdahl says. "It was pretty amazing—when we got to Puerto Rico on one of our earlier scouts, we were standing on top of the building Falcon stands on at the film's opening, and we were floored at how much it mirrored the research we had done on Lagos."

Due to its striking similarities, the Visual Effects team decided to use the location for background replacements. "We shot a plate unit down in Puerto Rico with drones and helicopters and camera trucks," Dan Deleeuw says. "We had numerous people scanning and photographing tons and tons of buildings with a lot of tactile texture and character, and used those in post-production to replace the backgrounds outside the Civic Center in Atlanta. All the people you see in the cars on the streets were practical in Atlanta, but the buildings behind them are all the plates we shot down in Puerto Rico."

CHAPTER ONE: SHOWDOWN IN LAGOS

"It's a little run-down, a little unclean," Paterson says. "It isn't the highly sanitized, immaculate facility that you might find in the United States, the UK, or Australia. It's a bit more edgy and potentially dangerous. If something were to leak out of here, it wouldn't be good for anybody."

Marek Okon keyframe.

John Eaves concept art.

John Eaves concept art.

Marek Okon keyframe.

CHAPTER ONE: SHOWDOWN IN LAGOS

"We built this set that we called 'the exploding corridor' in the same facility as the laboratories, the idea being that Cap would run down while Crossbones' men were firing at him with RPGs," Paterson says. "So we'd cut inside the hallway as we rigged it to explode, and then cut back to the outside to see them firing the guns. It was a really fun setup that we had very limited takes to accomplish due to the fact the set was being destroyed around him. Of course, Cap survives because of his strength and the shield, and he rolls out the end of the corridor, which leads into the back of the facility, which then leads into the Lagos marketplace."

Marek Okon keyframe.

"Originally I pictured it being a much bigger facility, as it had more screen time in early drafts," Paterson says. "As the script was refined, certain things got cut down, so there were elements we didn't actually build in the end."

CHAPTER ONE SHOWDOWN IN LAGOS

55

Maciej Kuciara concept art.

Manuel Plank-Jorge concept art.

"Lagos—the biggest city in Nigeria and one of the biggest cities in Africa, I think—is very overcrowded," Paterson says. "It gained its independence from Britain in the '60s, and so what we were looking for were buildings that were from the '60s that evoked that kind of period and were also a bit run-down. It also needed to be a compound with multiple facets that our heroes and villains could fight through and around."

CHAPTER ONE: SHOWDOWN IN LAGOS

Manuel Plank-Jorge concept art.

Manuel Plank-Jorge keyframe.

The fight spills out of the Institute for Infectious Diseases and into a nearby marketplace. "Originally there was going to be a big chase through the streets, but there weren't really good streets in Atlanta that felt anything like Lagos," Paterson says. "Instead, we set the chase in a marketplace. We were really lucky to find this space between a railway line and the railway headquarters from 50 years ago. There was this big parking area where we could do what we needed, more or less. We had a lot of reference for signage and set dressing going in, and the artists did some beautiful renderings that gave an account of what we were going to be building in that space. Of course, the Visual Effects team would come in and create the backdrop behind the market to unify this 'shantytown' feel."

Marek Okon concept art.

The turmoil in the overcrowded marketplace escalates the chase's already high stakes, reminding the audience of the human impact of Crossbones' threat. "I wanted to create the feeling that this was only a small part of an enormous market," Paterson says. "So what you're seeing is maybe 10 percent of what's actually there. There are hundreds of people in and around there—the idea that Crossbones could unleash this bioweapon amongst them is a devastating idea."

Marek Okon concept art.

CHAPTER ONE: SHOWDOWN IN LAGOS

Marek Okon keyframe.

Super heroes fight to prevent death and devastation. But despite their best efforts, disaster seems to follow the Avengers, and their actions are starting to have worldwide ramifications. "The opening scene in Lagos ends up being the straw that breaks the camel's back," Producer and Marvel Studios President Kevin Feige explains. "Captain America's team stops Crossbones from getting this bioweapon, which he would've used or sold and would have created hundreds of thousands of casualties. In stopping him, there's an explosion triggered by Scarlet Witch, and about a dozen people are killed. Secretary of State Thaddeus Ross storms into the Avengers' facility and acknowledges that while the world owes the Avengers a great debt, there's been a lot of damage and a lot of cleanup afterwards. There is a worldwide feeling of tension—people are nervous about the fact the Avengers are running around making their own decisions without any oversight by the world governments."

The solution? The Sokovia Accords, named after the country Ultron lifted and dropped out of the sky in Marvel's *Avengers: Age of Ultron*. The Accords come to the Avengers with signatures from the leaders of 117 countries, including Wakanda, who demand the heroes report to a newly organized UN branch that will oversee their future activities. The discord caused by the ramifications of the Sokovia Accords draws battle lines among the Avengers.

Rodney Fuentebella concept art.

STARK HONORS PRESENTATION

Jamie Rama concept art.

Jamie Rama concept art.

AVENGERS COMPOUND

THE
SOKOVIA ACCORDS

FRAMEWORK for the REGISTRATION
AND
DEPLOYMENT
OF
ENHANCED INDIVIDUALS

Registered by the United Kingdom of Great Britain, Austria, Germany, Russia
Italy, France, Northern Ireland, and the United States of America

Monica Fedrick concept art.

Tony Stark and Secretary of State Thaddeus Ross confront the team to deliver the Sokovia Accords edict at the newly established Avengers Compound, first seen at the conclusion of Marvel's *Avengers: Age of Ultron*. "[Directors] Joe and Anthony [Russo] wanted to create a cool, slightly industrial space that was also utilitarian," Production Designer Owen Paterson says. "It had personality, kind of like a frat house for super heroes. They wanted a space where you could live—you would come down the corridor to a common room, get yourself some breakfast or lunch, sit down at the table and get a briefing for a mission, and then head outside to the Quinjet and be gone."

Marek Okon concept art.

Marek Okon concept art.

CHAPTER TWO: THE SOKOVIA ACCORDS

"We were able to access a really great building in Atlanta, Georgia," Paterson says. "It was a brand-new building, and they were just moving into it. This turned out to work to our advantage, as Joe and Anthony wanted to embrace the industrial feel of the exposed air conditioning and lighting while injecting some color pops with the furniture. We wanted to add in some personal effects to give it an even more believable, homelike feel. There's also a certain sharpness to it through the use of glass. The bottom line was that it wasn't a huge facility, but there's a training area, workshops, and more—I imagine on other movies it will be explored even further."

In the comics, Wanda and Vision shared a tumultuous romance. "It's still very early, but it's an arc we are hinting at," says Executive Producer and Head of Physical Production Victoria Alonso. "Vision and Wanda are in similar situations: They're both overwhelmed by the world around them and are learning how to adapt. Vision is a bit more pragmatic, and Wanda is more of a wildcard, but it's their differences that really make them an interesting match. Putting them on opposite teams—Wanda with Cap, and Vision with Tony—led to some great moments that equally challenge and strengthen their feelings for one another."

Maciej Kuciara concept art.

CHAPTER TWO: THE SOKOVIA ACCORDS

STEVE'S OFFICE

Some areas of Avengers Compound, like Steve Rogers' office, were designed with the express purpose of establishing location and tone, Owen Paterson says. "Much like the rest of the facility, there is a lot of glass in here—in this case a number of large-scale windows. This offered us the ability to see out into the environment a little—to offer a sense of where they were and what's around them outside."

Manuel Plank-Jorge concept art.

CHAPTER TWO: THE SOKOVIA ACCORDS

77

THE VISION

Still acclimating to life with the Avengers, Vision isn't human—nor is he a mere robot. The fine line between the two inspired his wardrobe for Marvel's *Captain America: Civil War*. "Vision wants to feel comfortable around all of these humans he is seeing every day at the Avengers Compound," Costume Designer Judianna Makovsky says. "Alternatively, I think he wants people to feel more comfortable around him, so we decided to put him in plain clothes for some sequences in the film."

Ryan Meinerding concept art.

Mariano Diaz concept art.

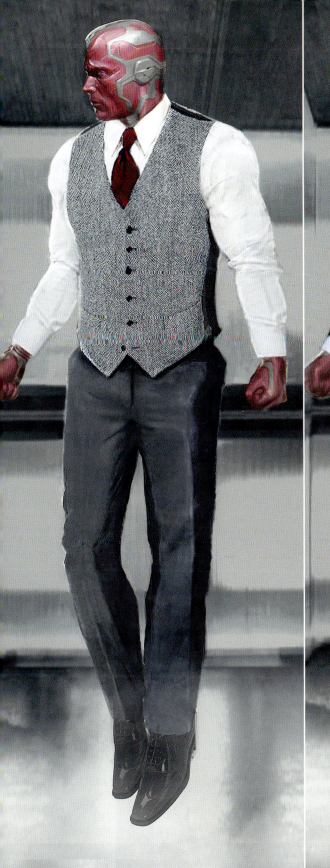
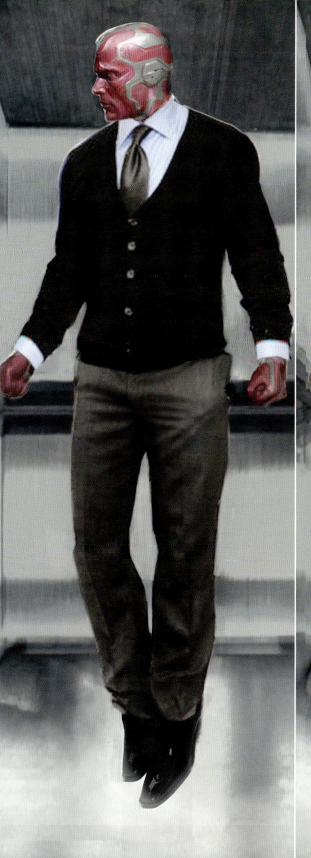
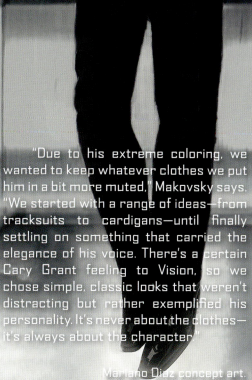

CHAPTER TWO: THE SOKOVIA ACCORDS

"Due to his extreme coloring, we wanted to keep whatever clothes we put him in a bit more muted," Makovsky says. "We started with a range of ideas—from tracksuits to cardigans—until finally settling on something that carried the elegance of his voice. There's a certain Cary Grant feeling to Vision, so we chose simple, classic looks that weren't distracting but rather exemplified his personality. It's never about the clothes—it's always about the character."

Mariano Diaz concept art.

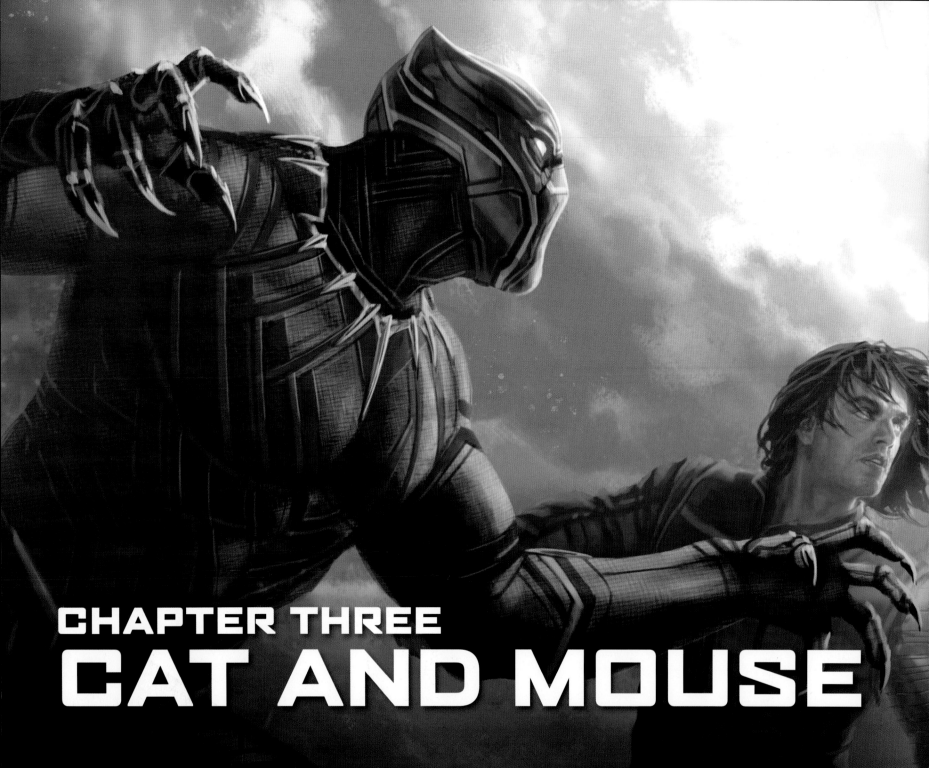

CHAPTER THREE
CAT AND MOUSE

When the UN meets to vote on the Sokovia Accords, a tragic bombing ratchets up the tension among the Avengers—and evidence points to Captain America's comrade-turned-assassin Bucky Barnes, a.k.a. the Winter Soldier, as the culprit. A relentless three-way chase to track him down ensues—involving Tony Stark, working with the world's governments; T'Challa, a.k.a. Black Panther, fueled by the desire for vengeance; and Steve Rogers, beguiled by loyalty and friendship. Without a doubt, this film represents Captain America's most emotionally demanding installment in the Marvel Cinematic Universe. The Russo brothers attribute Steve Rogers' emotional breadth to a blend of the script with actor Chris Evans' own life. "It's fascinating working on these movies, because no one's really done this other than maybe the Bond films and the Harry Potter films, where you've extended story and serialized storytelling out over this many years and this many films, and had the same actors playing the same characters for this long," Director Joe Russo explains. "There are nuances and the subtleties that they find every time they play the part, and also as they grow as human beings, and I think there's a real gravitas and maturity that Cap has.

"This is reflective of where Chris is in his life. He's an incredibly technically gifted actor. He's amazing with physicality, with understanding where the cameras are. He's fantastic with stunts, which allows us to use him a lot in the movie to do his own fighting and do his own stunts. I think that adds a level of realism that we crave. I find that he's successfully in our minds taken the character from someone who is taking orders from a structure, an institution, in the first movie, to someone who is now giving orders as a kind of revolutionary. It's a really interesting arc for somebody named Captain America."

It was the production team's job to mirror that emotional scope through carefully structured visual cues that bring a tactile resonance to the film.

BUCKY BARNES / THE WINTER SOLDIER

Bucky Barnes has been lying low since the events of Marvel's *Captain America: The Winter Soldier*. To accompany his intention to blend in, the Winter Soldier's overall design initiative fully embraced a less-is-more approach.

"I've worked on Bucky's looks since *Captain America: The First Avenger*, so I've been very interested in continuing to define the evolution of his look," Head of Visual Development Ryan Meinerding says. "In this movie, he is in hiding, which meant stripping away the vestures of being a super hero and placing him in a casual setting. The jacket he rips the sleeve off to reveal the silver arm is his look for the majority of the movie. It's slightly more heightened and is meant to represent a newer version of his Winter Soldier costume. Instead of having buttons running down one side of his torso, its design details are more squared."

Ryan Meinerding concept art.

Ryan Meinerding concept art.

CHAPTER THREE: CAT AND MOUSE

Ryan Meinerding concept art.

CHAPTER THREE: CAT AND MOUSE

"Bucky's costumes in this film are based on adaptability," Costume Designer Judianna Makovsky says. "We needed to make sure his looks made sense, with him being on the run and all. I always want to create a backstory for where each character could have gotten their clothing. Bucky isn't in a position to have a superhero costume—it needs to feel pieced together from here and there."

Ryan Meinerding concept art.

T'CHALLA / BLACK PANTHER

Since his first comic-book appearance in *Fantastic Four #52* in 1966, Black Panther has been equally powerful and enigmatic. Translating T'Challa's iconic prowess from comic to screen was a task Ryan Meinerding approached with fervent excitement. "I tend to like to design the 'men-of-action' of the Marvel Cinematic Universe. I find the ones I'm drawn to are the more physical ones, the ones who specialize in hand-to-hand combat. Panther's silhouette throughout the comics has always been lithe, and because the costume is primarily black with muscle shapes, the challenge with this one was trying to find a way to translate something that's simple to a real-world setting with enough texture and detail to not just be a man in a black leotard. I was trying to come up with ways of having the suit constructed that the audience wouldn't understand—it's meant to be woven together in ways that are nearly impossible to achieve in a practical setting, and therefore make it feel like it's from a culture that's way more advanced than ours."

Ryan Meinerding concept art.

"The overall concept is that it's a woven suit—on a more granular level, there is Vibranium woven into the fabric," Meinerding says. "This Vibranium thread would provide a silver sheen so that when it catches the light, it would glisten a bit. From there we tried to create a design language for patterns to fit very subtly into the hard Vibranium pieces that are woven through the suit."

Ryan Meinerding concept art.

CHAPTER THREE: CAT AND MOUSE

"With the helmet, [Concept Illustrator] Andy Park had done a first pass with some design lines that the Russo brothers mentioned they wanted to keep," Meinerding says. "That's where I started. I tried to break up the mask even more to hopefully evoke the tribal abstraction of a panther mixed with a man while also representing a high-tech society. For instance, there are carvings on the mask, but they're carved in such a precise way that it would take a high level of technology to achieve. For the eyes, we were trying to replicate something that felt like when a cat's eye catches light at night time—a subtle, metallic look."

Ryan Meinerding concept art.

"The Russo brothers were very interested in having Panther be able to fight with claws, but not be tied to fighting with them all the time—the idea being that he could retract them and still have a regular fistfight with someone," Meinerding says. "So there are Vibranium claws that can extend and retract, and he also has pieces of Vibranium worked into his knuckles so when he fights he's just as formidable with simple punches."

Ryan Meinerding concept art.

CHAPTER THREE: CAT AND MOUSE

"In this pass on the design I was focusing on showing how the Vibranium weave could work as a costume mimicking human anatomy," Concept Artist Jerad Marantz says. "Conceptually, the hardest thing about this is that the only other example of this metal that we see in the cinematic universe is Captain America's shield. My solution was to make the costume a combination of rigid plates and Vibranium woven strips that emulate the character's muscles."

Jerad Marantz concept art.

CHAPTER THREE: CAT AND MOUSE

Andy Park concept art.

"My focus when doing designs for Black Panther was on creating a costume that conveyed strength, agility, and technology in a subtle way—all while being reminiscent of his comic-book look." Lead Visual Development Concept Illustrator Andy Park says. "It's a suit that is actually very high-tech, but that technology would be literally sewn into the suit as opposed to an exterior shell like the Iron Man suit."

Andy Park concept art.

CHAPTER THREE: CAT AND MOUSE

"A lot of what I played with was creating accents and sheens throughout his body to convey that the Vibranium was built within the production of the suit," Park says. "Along with the technological aspect, I tried to infuse a tribal look that is the foundation of his look from his comic-book origins."

Andy Park concept art.

93

JAMES RHODES / WAR MACHINE

War Machine's aesthetic in *Civil War* represents a departure from his slim, streamlined appearance in Marvel's *Avengers: Age of Ultron*. "We wanted to alter the form language and overall silhouette to make sure Iron Man and War Machine felt different," Concept Artist Phil Saunders says. "We started out using some car analogies—if we were going to use Ferrari or Lamborghini language on Iron Man, we'd make War Machine more like the walking Humvee or the walking tank. This means a lot more planar, a little less integrated—a little less of all the lines lining up and flowing the way you have on the Mark 46 Iron Man suit. Overall, I used much more rectangular, bulky shapes."

Phil Saunders concept art.

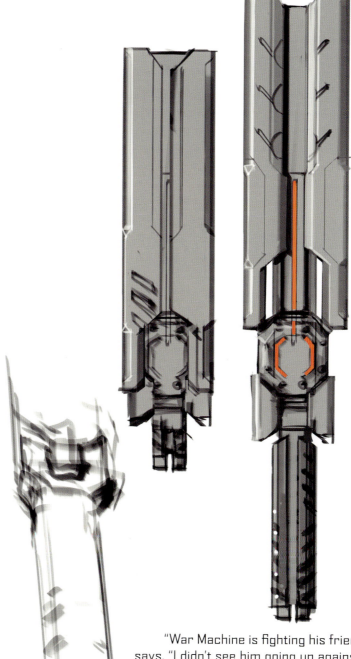

CHAPTER THREE: CAT AND MOUSE

"War Machine is fighting his friends," Saunders says. "I didn't see him going up against Black Widow or Ant-Man and unloading with a chain gun. These are people, humans—they don't have bulletproof skin. They were trying to detain each other, incapacitate each other, not aiming to kill. This stun baton was a great non-lethal crowd-control-type weapon."

Phil Saunders concept art.

War Machine's baton also allowed for a little fun in an otherwise serious moment. "I thought it was interesting to see this large piece on his back come up and deploy something that looks like his gun, and aim at a character—they're going 'uh-oh'—and then he grabs what you think is the barrel and pulls it out, and it's this big baton," Saunders says. "The baton would then open up a bit, charge up, and deliver some real 'shock value.'"

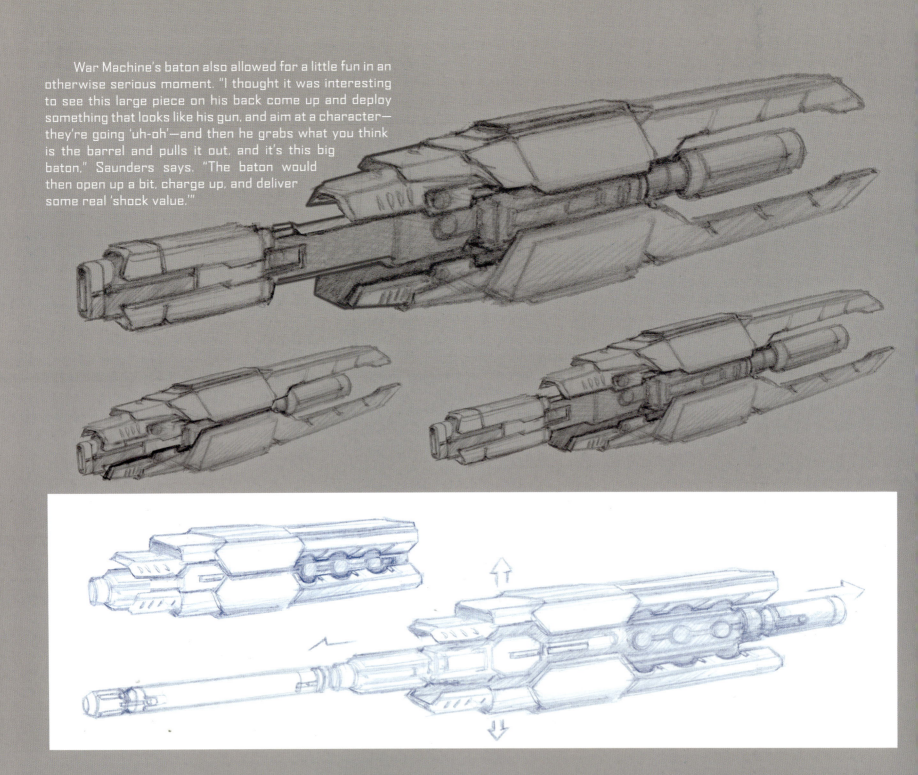

John Eaves concept art.

CHAPTER THREE: CAT AND MOUSE

Before the design was finalized, Saunders explored additional concepts. "There was a conscious intent in the early passes to make him more authoritarian," Saunders says. "He and Tony Stark are representing the side of the government and taking control of the super heroes. A lot of the reference that I looked at was crowd-control police and S.W.A.T. uniforms, masks, and body armor."

Phil Saunders concept art.

THE BUCHAREST CHASE
STORYBOARDS BY DARRIN DENLINGER

The epic Bucharest chase begins in the seemingly mundane, yet methodically organized, apartment of Bucky Barnes. "We wanted to put him in an environment that told a story in as short of a time as possible," Executive Producer Nate Moore says. "There're a lot of different ways you can be 'off the grid'—there's the cabin-in-the-woods version; there's the desert-island version. We thought it would be more interesting if Bucky was hiding somewhere in plain sight. Sometimes you can be more anonymous in a big city. It allowed him a weird autonomy that felt different than the expected. We had taken a research trip out to Germany and were looking for locations that would double as Romania, and we found a really interesting Depression-era town that was very industrial, and we based the look of the building off that. It was one of those very gray places where the sky always feels overcast, and everything is kind of used, and there's soot on the walls—that kind of textural detail was really interesting."

With that real-life inspiration, the production team built a set that told Bucky's story through small details. "The apartment itself is in a corner lot and very high up in the air, which allows him a vantage point to see people coming," Moore says. "We liked the idea that his door, which actually plays plot-wise in the apartment, is reinforced steel—it's not something you can break open like wood. There's a false floor where he's hidden a go-pack near the kitchen. The general idea of the interior of the apartment was to give him a lot of nooks and crannies that would be useful for someone who wants to appear to be normal but still has weapon caches stored in a lot of different places."

Maciej Kuciara concept art.

Maciej Kuciara concept art.

Concept Artist Maciej Kuciara worked with Production Designer Owen Paterson and the Russo brothers to capture the overall tone of Bucky's apartment. "I generally try to approach my illustrations so they look and feel like key moments straight from the final cut of the film," Kuciara says. "That level of realism gives that extra fidelity I feel can help production designers and directors realize their vision with extreme clarity. Story always comes first—so before approaching any integration of characters into my concepts, I would talk to Owen and figure out what we're after. Everything surrounding Bucky and the other characters would have to visually support that storytelling moment."

CHAPTER THREE: CAT AND MOUSE

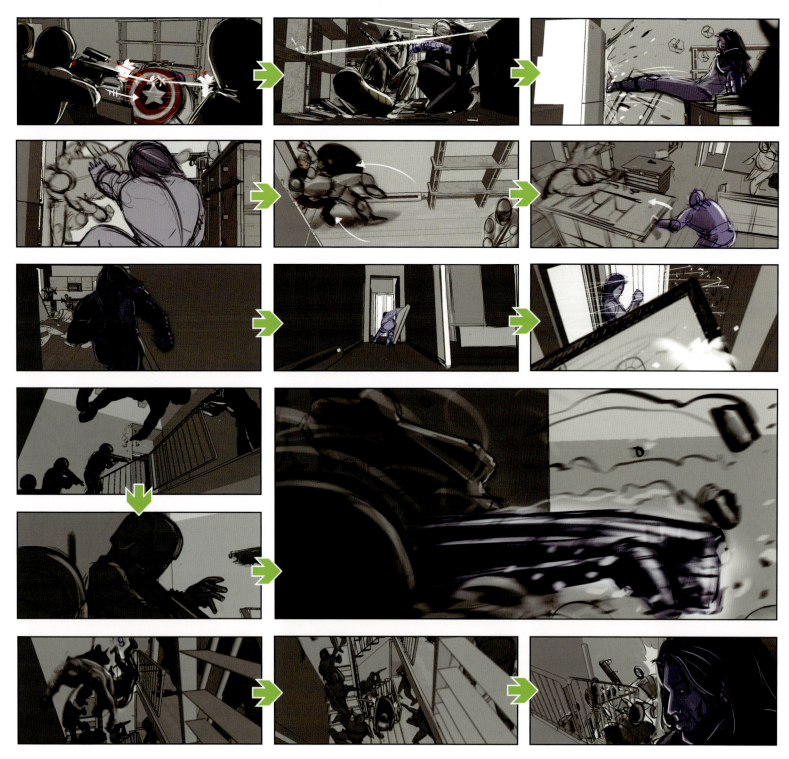

"Marvel's *Captain America: Civil War* was such a unique experience for me because Joe and Anthony Russo brought me—and the other main board artist, Anthony Liberatore—into the project incredibly early in the process," Storyboard Artist Darrin Denlinger says. "In those early days, we had many meetings with the core creative group, really poring through just an early outline from writers Chris Markus and Stephen McFeely, hashing out beat sheets, and pitching action ideas. This is where the Bucky chase sequence really took shape, creating a narrative framework to hang all the amazing ideas that were being generated from everyone. From there, it was a matter of picking and choosing the best stuff and, once photos from the initial Berlin location scout came in, focusing in on the beats that could really exploit those wonderful locales."

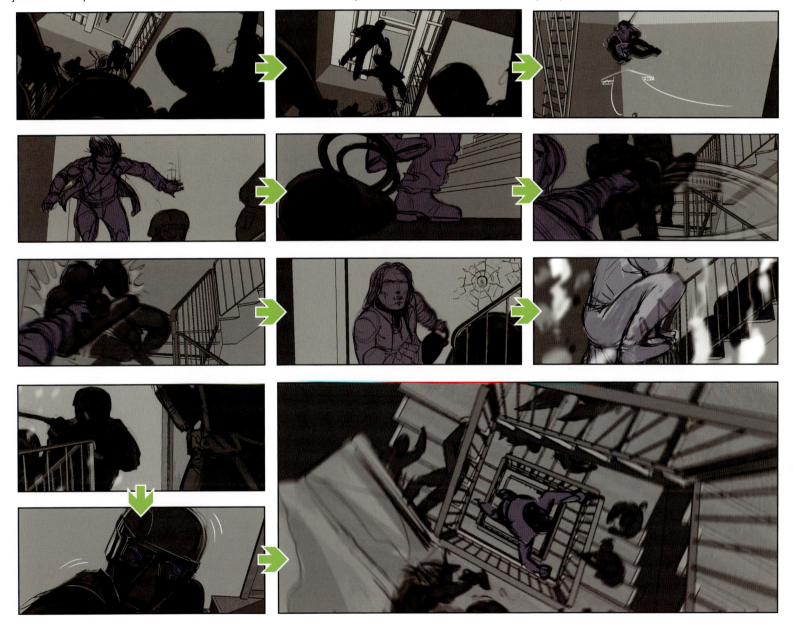

CHAPTER THREE: CAT AND MOUSE

103

Maciej Kuciara concept art.

CHAPTER THREE: CAT AND MOUSE

The chaotic fight moves from the interior of Bucky's apartment to the stairwell outside his door. As Moore explains, Bucky has mapped out the entire place—his living arrangement is a series of calculated choices: "When you're living off the grid, you've got to have everything figured out. Even though his apartment is rigged for an easy escape, he also purposefully chose the corner unit at the top of a stairwell with restrictive access. This means guys can only come at him one at a time, easily allowing him to tear through them. He didn't want to be in a wide-open courtyard where he could be easily overwhelmed."

CHAPTER THREE: CAT AND MOUSE

Maciej Kuciara concept art.

107

Maciej Kuciara concept art.

CHAPTER THREE: CAT AND MOUSE

109

The entire high-stakes sequence explodes when Black Panther enters the fray, Denlinger says. "We had been going for quite a while before the bomb dropped that we were gonna introduce Panther in the film. I was thrilled that I would get a shot at T'Challa's first appearance in costume. I knew that the majority of the fight would be ultimately handled by the amazing stunt crew lead by Sam Hargrave and James Young, so I focused on making his intro shot as dynamic as possible. I also wanted to quickly get across some important story points regarding Panther and his Vibranium-enhanced costume. Conceived to be as indestructible as Cap's shield, it would allow T'Challa to be aggressive and bold with his technique with little fear of injury. He could hold onto the bumper of an SUV and ski behind it during a high-speed chase or walk through mini-gun helicopter fire. Additionally, one of the most important qualities of Vibranium is its ability to absorb kinetic energy. This would allow Panther to stand strong against a devastating metal-arm punch from the Winter Soldier."

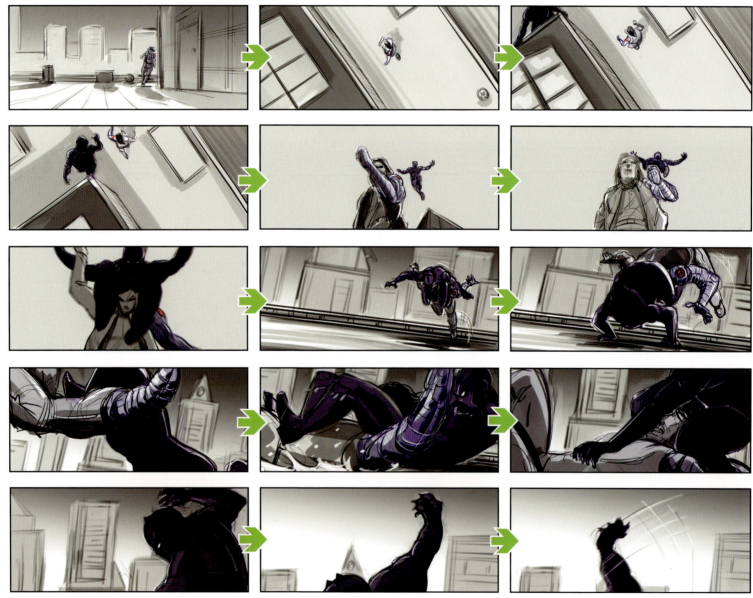

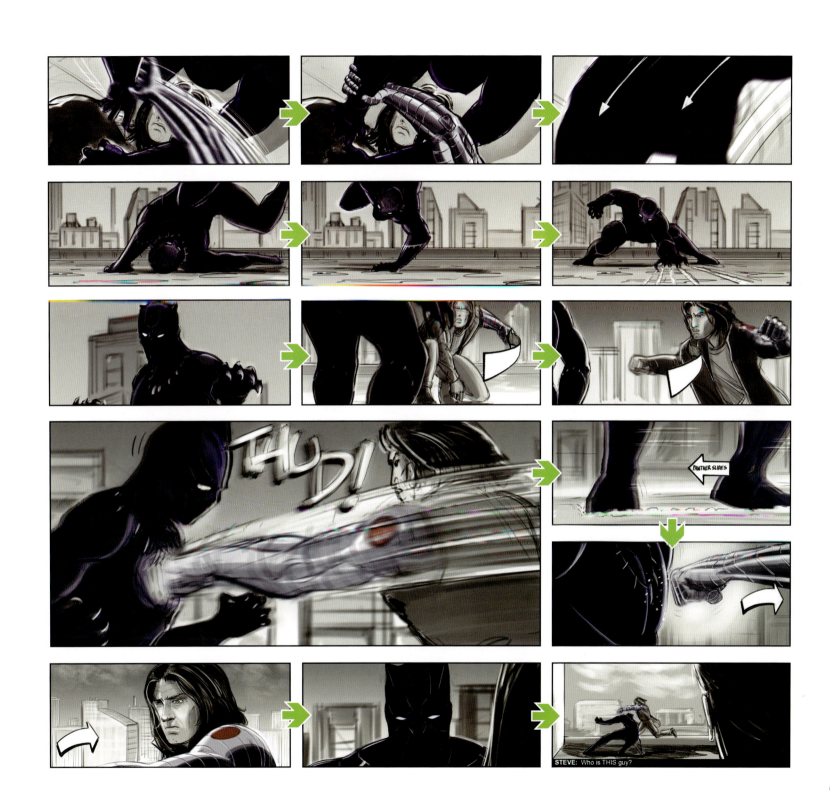

STORYBOARD OVERHEADS
BY TONY LIBERATORE

Storyboard Artist Tony Liberatore helped plan the sequence. "I took on most of the bike-and-car-chase work once Second Unit Director Spiro Razatos came aboard," Liberatore explains. "Spiro had a lot of creative input, as well." Along with traditional storyboards, Liberatore created overhead diagrams detailing how the action would play out, offering a broader view of the intricate sequence. "A lot of the details of this particular scene were worked out early on between the Russos, Christopher Markus and Stephen McFeely, and the very talented Darrin Denlinger," Liberatore says. "As I started boarding, lots of new ideas would just organically pop up. Getting the timing down for the tunnel explosion was a real challenge. There was so much simultaneous character action happening during that beat."

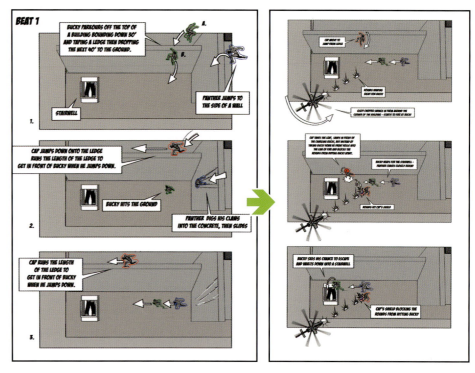

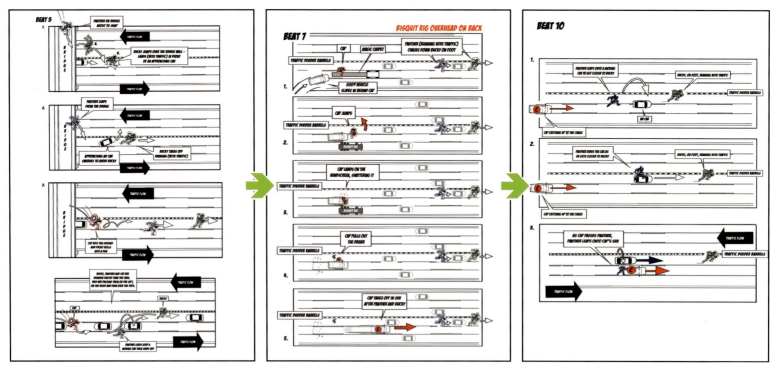

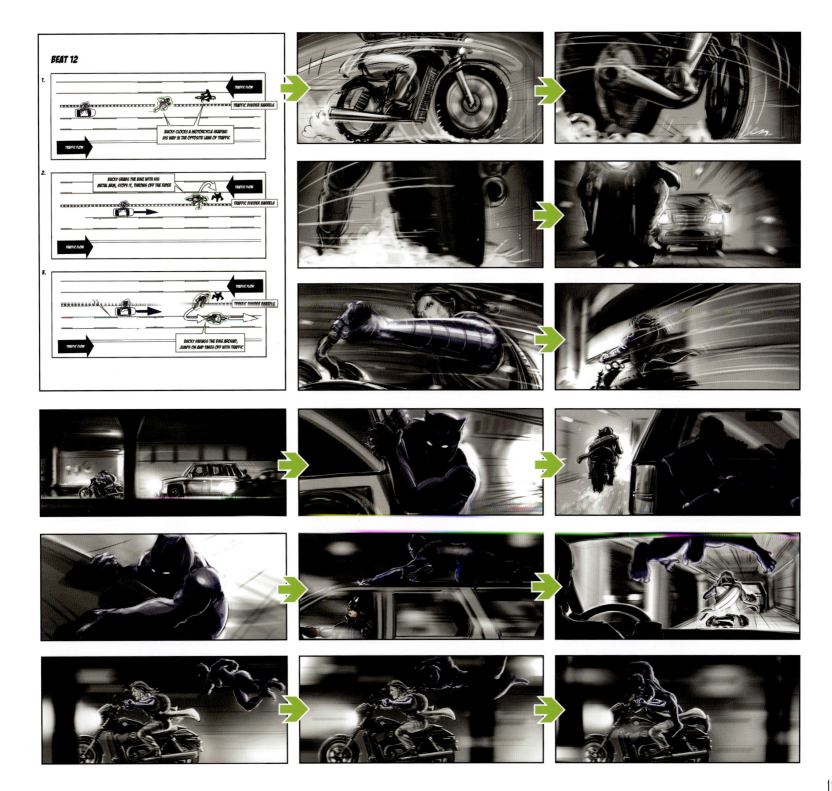

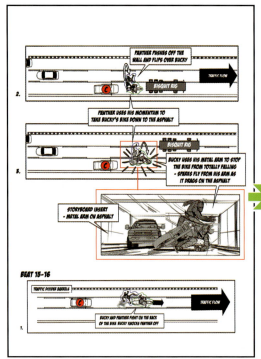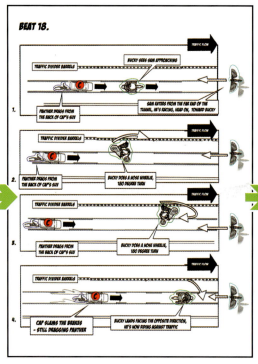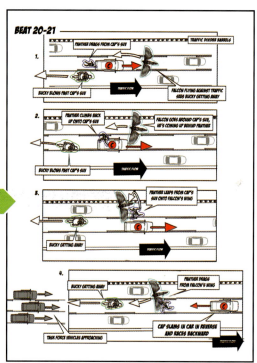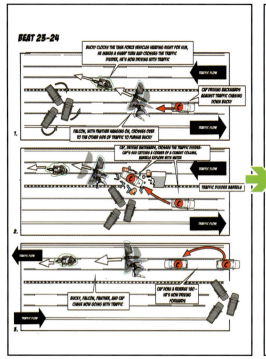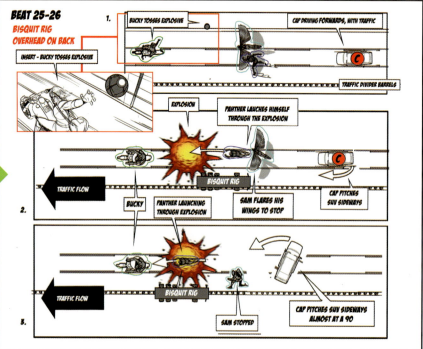

"I was always mindful of each characters' strengths and attributes, and thinking of ways to utilize them organically within the scene," Liberatore says. "For example, the Panther/Bucky fight on the motorcycle was a great opportunity to show off Black Panther's agility by having him try to flip Bucky's bike over. While on the back of Bucky's bike, he'd push off the tunnel wall and vault over Bucky. This led to Bucky using his metal arm to keep the bike from totally falling on its side."

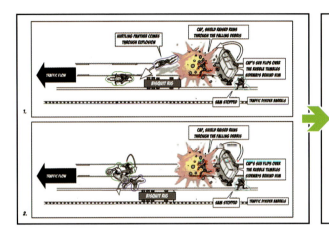
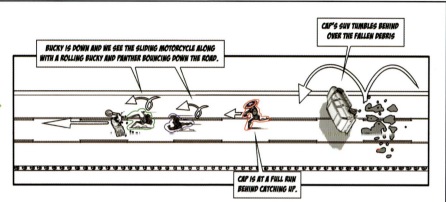
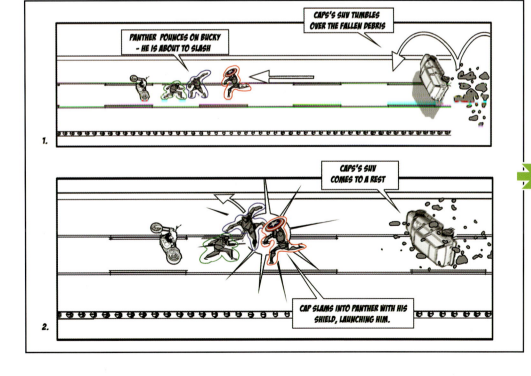
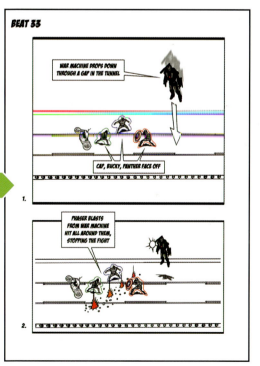

"I have a huge amount of trouble illustrating heroes fighting heroes," Ryan Meinerding says. "I have such an affinity for all of the characters—it's hard for me to figure out how to frame action when I very specifically have to say who is winning or who is better at fighting in this particular moment. For this keyframe of Black Panther scratching Cap's shield, I was using one of my favorite comic-book covers by Mike Zeck [from 1986's *Captain America Annual #8*] of Wolverine scratching Cap's shield as inspiration. The frame is favoring Black Panther's body and the forward motion of his attack, but Cap is able to take the hit and still keep his head forward, which I think is a cool statement: Cap's not really scared of this dangerous attack."

Ryan Meinerding concept art.

CHAPTER THREE: CAT AND MOUSE

CHAPTER FOUR
MIND GAMES

With Bucky Barnes in custody, and Steve Rogers and his crew in holding, a stranger with a nefarious plan takes advantage of the situation. Armed only with a small red book, he sits down for a face-to-face with Bucky under the guise of a psychologist. According to Director Anthony Russo, this stranger—whom we come to know as Helmut Zemo—was morally constructed to be both right and wrong, much like the other characters in the film. "It was very important for us to give Zemo a valid point of view," Russo says. "That was the heart of how we constructed the narrative and the storytelling of this movie—every character has some validity to their point of view.

We've always been more excited by villains who do have a valid point of view. We've always found them scarier and more threatening than a villain you can write off as just crazy or unhinged. Zemo is very dangerous and scary—while at the same time being grounded in a relatable way with raw human emotions and experience." It's fitting, then, that the unstable Zemo sets former villain Bucky Barnes back on the warpath, driving away the very humanity he's been fighting to regain since the events of Marvel's *Captain America: The Winter Soldier*. All it takes are a few trigger words from a red codebook, and the Winter Soldier is back on autopilot.

SHARON CARTER / AGENT 13

Since S.H.I.E.L.D.'s collapse in Marvel's *Captain America: The Winter Soldier*, Agent 13—Sharon Carter—has been working as a liaison for Interpol. "She is a government employee, and I wanted to make sure whatever we put her in accentuated that," Costume Designer Judianna Makovsky says. "We custom-made her jacket to ensure the right fit, the right color, and the classically beautiful style the Russo brothers wanted to convey. She isn't an outrageous personality, so keeping her overall aesthetic subdued was key."

Nathan Schroeder concept art.

Christian Cordella concept art.

CHAPTER FOUR: MIND GAMES

TASKFORCE HEADQUARTERS

Manuel Plank-Jorge concept art.

The majority of the interiors for Taskforce Headquarters were built on sound stages in Atlanta, Georgia. "They're really unique, complex sets," Production Designer Owen Paterson says. "There's a great ceiling that expands over this glass-laden conference room in the center. You're really not sure if Steve is a prisoner or whether he can freely leave this glass box inside of another box."

Nathan Schroeder concept art.

CHAPTER FOUR: MIND GAMES

"There's also a lot of exposition that takes place within these sets," Paterson says. "I wanted to give an opportunity for interest in what's happening in the background. So if you had 20 or 30 screens out and around the perimeter of these glass walls, and people at computer desks, and you were inside the glass box, there was always going to be a reflection happening here and there. That was the aesthetic I was going for. It was visually interesting without being distracting."

Nathan Schroeder concept art.

While Tony and Steve argue about the Sokovia Accords in the conference area, Bucky's containment unit is transferred to the lower levels of Taskforce Headquarters. The sterile, metallic hallways and loading bay were meant to emphasize the government building's scale, as well as its power. "The environments that I did for the film were paintings done over the existing location where we'd potentially be shooting," Concept Artist Paul Ozzimo says. "I was asked to add some stainless door elements and some floor graphics to make everything feel more official."

Paul Ozzimo concept art.

"It was interesting to bring Cap back to Europe, where he began as a tool of American propaganda and then turned himself into a hero," Director Joe Russo says. "He's coming full circle in a way. Also, Europe has changed dramatically—Berlin, in particular. Now it's the heart of the European Union. When Bucky is captured in the film, he's brought to Berlin because it's where the intelligence is, and because GSG9 is behind his capture. So you have a real strong, modern German presence as a peacekeeping nation and as a powerhouse of Europe. That was important for us—to convey that reality. Everything's changed; Cap's changed."

CHAPTER FOUR: MIND GAMES

Paul Ozzimo concept art.

Paul Ozzimo concept art.

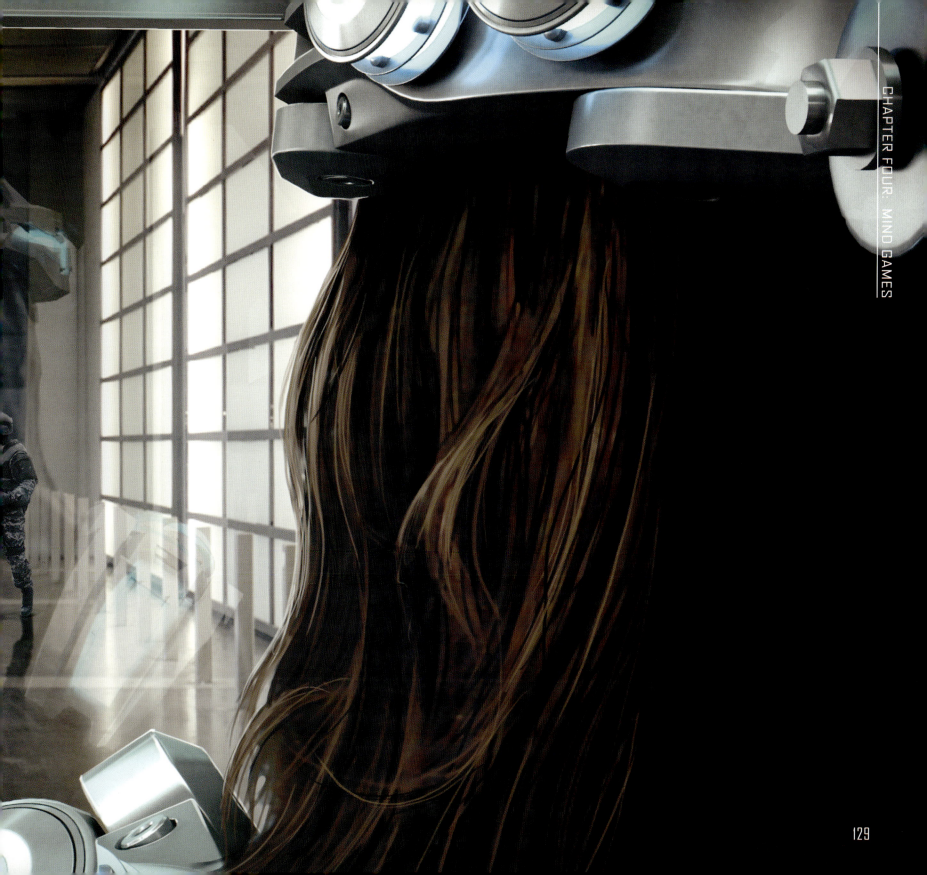

Rodney Fuentebella concept art.

Early passes for Bucky's containment chamber explored a variety of aesthetics. "I wanted these units to feel like he is an animal—caught in a trap—and even with all his strength, he wouldn't be able to escape," Concept Artist Rodney Fuentebella says. "I explored the use of high-tech, possibly Stark-tech, elements such as electrifying the outside bars. There's a level of empathy I think the audience will feel if the exterior of the cage seems dangerous. It's an interesting juxtaposition to put such an intensely powerful person into a situation that makes them seem helpless."

Rodney Fuentebella concept art.

John Eaves concept art.

Paul Ozzimo concept art.

The containment chamber is transported into the bowels of the facility, where Bucky awaits psychological evaluation. "The space is a bit like being in solitary confinement," Paterson says. "It's surrounded in concrete, which offered a desolate and somber atmosphere that mirrors Bucky's alienation. He's also very vulnerable here—it's a large, empty, open space, and he's on display. The design of the space is as inspired as the story we're trying to tell with the characters here."

WINTER SOLDIER CONTAINMENT CHAMBER

"The Winter Soldier is arguably the most dangerous criminal in the world, and this chamber really mirrors his intensity," says Executive Producer and Head of Physical Production Victoria Alonso. "With his metal arm, the necessary steps for containing him needed to be extreme. We created an electric pulse, administered by the chair, that would go through him every so often and keep him from using the arm. You couldn't just have him in a really strong chair with manacles because he's far stronger than that. The idea that the chair needs to be powered to keep Bucky at bay also plays into the story: When the power gets cut, the electric pulses stop, and suddenly he has the potential to escape."

Paul Ozzimo concept art.

"The shape of the chamber came from the idea of luggage—a massive luggage container that would be self-contained for a human," Owen Paterson says. "This means there would be air conditioning and air supply, and there was a power unit that would keep the manacles on his arms and legs. We had to keep in mind this was a mobile unit—this was going to go into an airplane; it had to be container sized. We wanted to make sure no human being would actually have to touch him or really interact with him once he was inside."

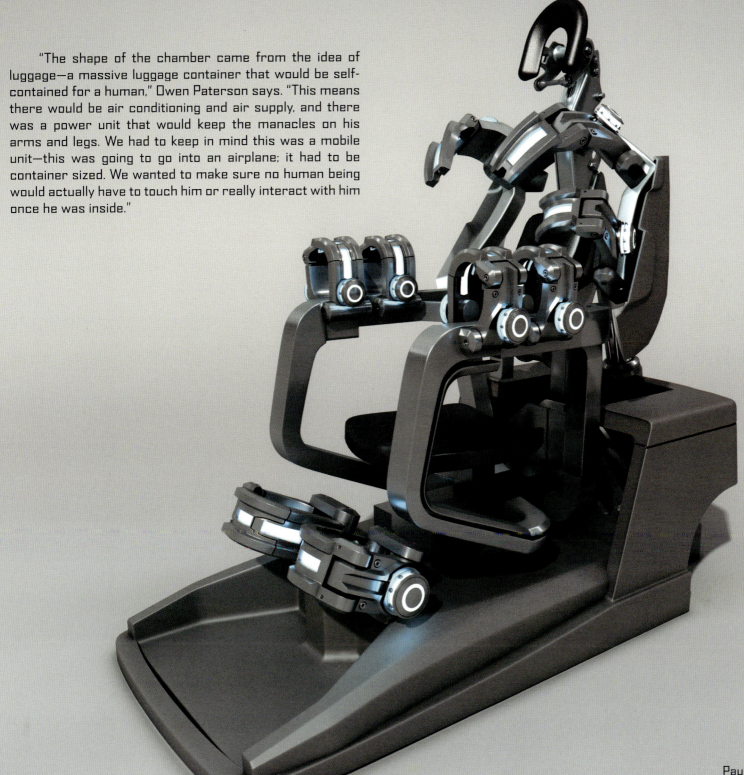

CHAPTER FOUR: MIND GAMES

Paul Ozzimo concept art.

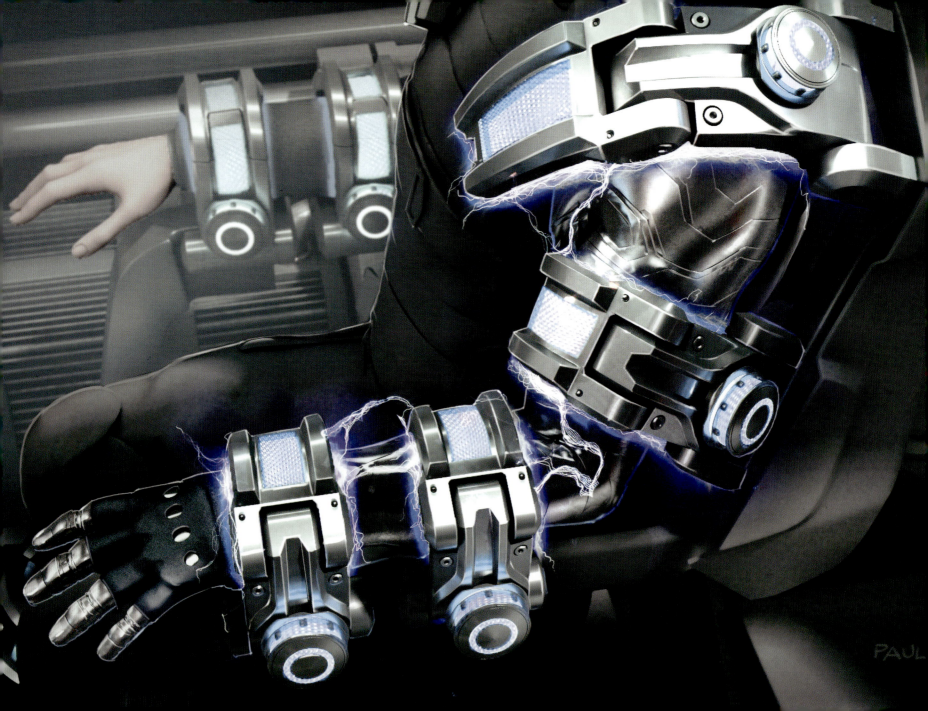

"The first project that I was given on the film was the 'Bucky container,'" Paul Ozzimo says. "The design was very much inspired by airline shipping containers, which are essentially rectangular shapes with the corners cut off to accommodate the curvature of an aircraft body. It also needed to feel very strong, so I wrapped it in a thick roll cage. Inside, Bucky is held in place by some hefty clamps that deliver a nice electrical charge to keep him still. The idea was to make those restraints look as strong as possible."

Paul Ozzimo concept art.

ESCAPE FROM TASKFORCE HEADQUARTERS

Andy Park keyframe.

Manuel Plank-Jorge concept art.

Manuel Plank-Jorge concept art.

CHAPTER FOUR: MIND GAMES

Bucky's journey during the course of *Civil War* is emotionally and physically complex, but actor Sebastian Stan embraced the challenge. "I was really excited when I read the script," Stan says. "I didn't really know where they were going to take it because the playing field was so open. They could've done anything with the character. But I was really happy as an actor because I got a chance to play a lot of different colors. The Winter Soldier is a little bit in the middle in this film. He sees flashes of Bucky Barnes and who he used to be; things are coming back to him. He's learning about himself—he's just no longer the same guy. He's always going to have that Winter Soldier sort of shadow over him going forward. I think what was fun about the script was that when you're reading, you never knew where he was going to swing—he might become the Winter Soldier, he might sort of be Bucky Barnes. So there was a lot of playing room there. That was fun."

WANDA COMPOUND BREAKOUT

Due to the incident in Lagos, Wanda is detained in Avengers Compound at Tony Stark's direction—and under Vision's watchful eye—until an explosion erupts outside, momentarily distracting Vision while Hawkeye attempts to extract Wanda. It's the first time we see the team members truly go head-to-head. "This scene was not scripted when I was called to work on the project," Storyboard Artist Richard Bennett Lamas says. "[Directors] Anthony and Joe [Russo] described it over the phone, and we exchanged some ideas, but there was a lot of freedom initially. The Russo brothers made very clear from the beginning that this scene was not only a good way to indicate who was taking which side, but also mainly to emphasize the internal struggle Wanda was going through. She didn't want to use her powers again since she felt responsible for the slaughter of innocent people early on in the film. The scene was supposed to have a crescendo vibe that would eventually end up with her unleashing her power to stop Vision from seriously harming Clint."

Marek Okon concept art.

CHAPTER FOUR: MIND GAMES

Marek Okon concept art.

STORYBOARDS
BY RICHARD BENNETT LAMAS

"Each character's strengths, skills, and personality dictated the chain of events," Bennett says. "Hawkeye is pretty much special ops, so he moves and operates as such—relying not only on his skills, but on weapons, as well. The goal was to make him almost invisible in the first half of the scene—cunning, to the point he could fool Vision and his arsenal of technology. The idea was to keep the suspense or mystery about who, or what, was intruding into the compound."

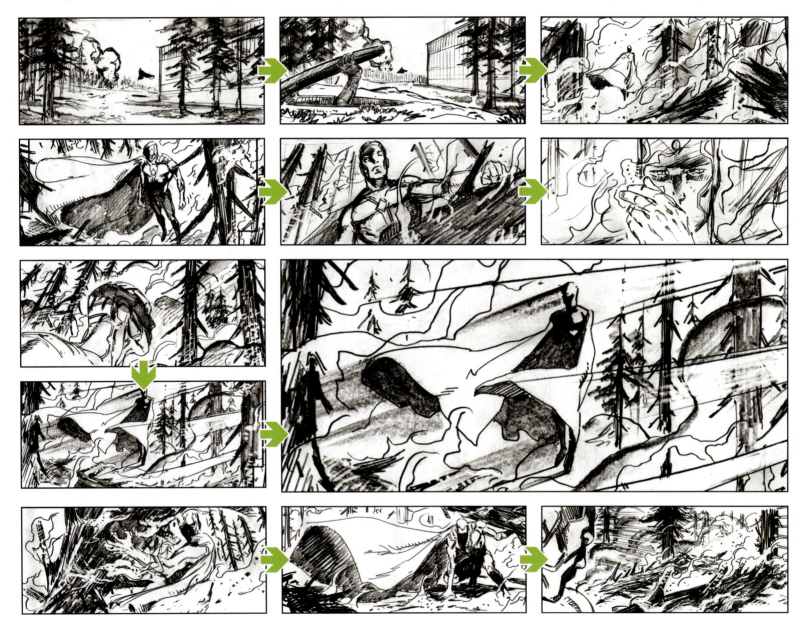

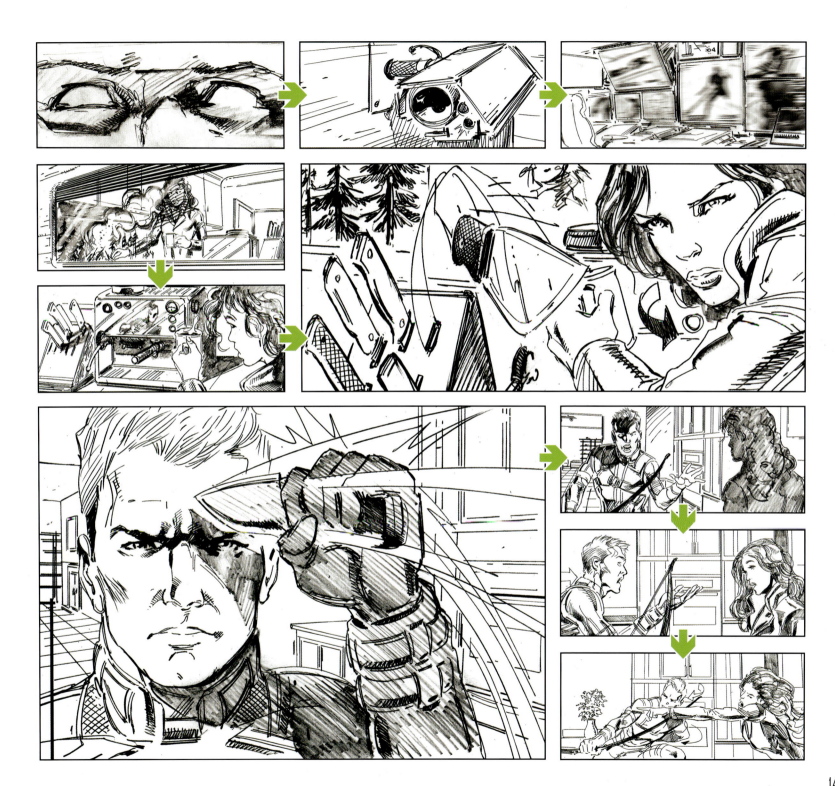

CHAPTER FOUR: MIND GAMES

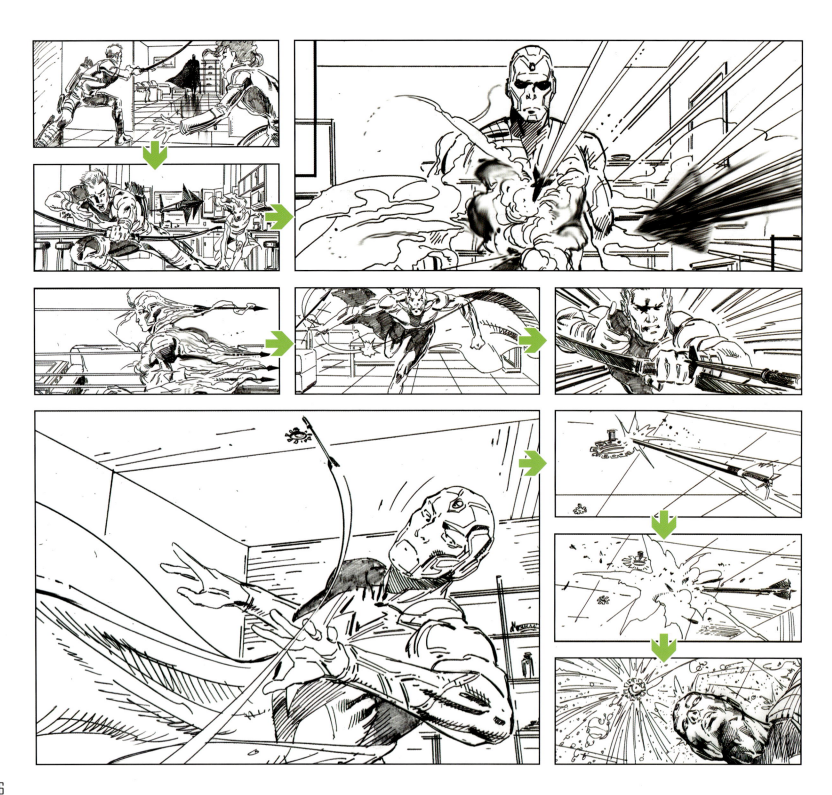

"Wanda was supposed to come off as insecure and conflicted in the beginning. Then in the end, she shows you really don't want to mess with her," Bennett says. "Vision was great, because of the character's creepy aspect. He's an android, yet he can change the molecular structure of his body. I like the element of contained or controlled power in Vision's archetype. It was a challenge, though, to depict Vision in a menacing way, yet not so violent that it seemed he might kill Hawkeye with his next move. And then again the scene—and the violence—had to escalate in order for Wanda to react."

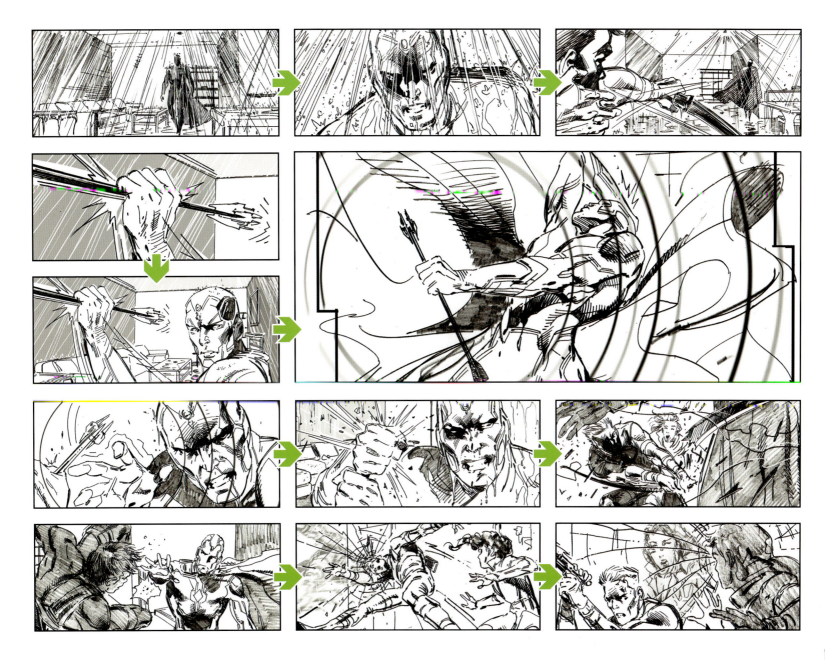

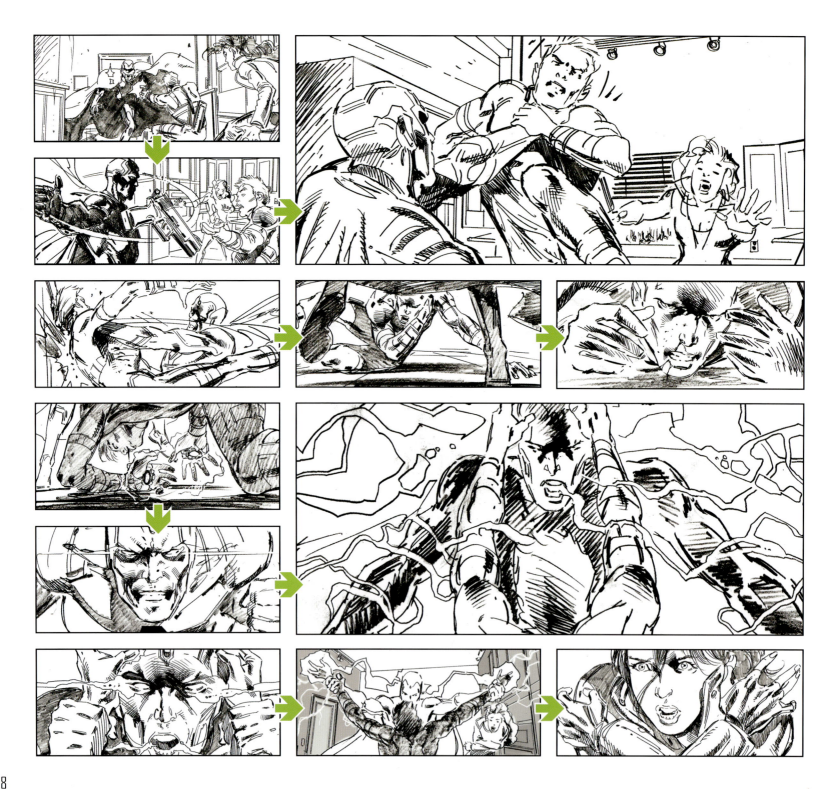

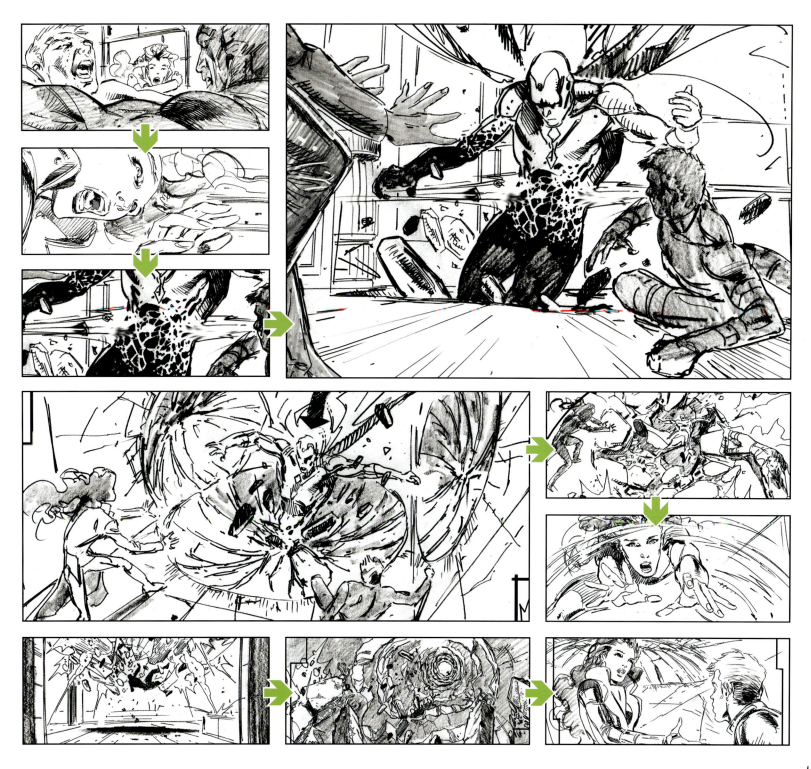

CHAPTER FOUR: MIND GAMES

CHAPTER FIVE
CIVIL WAR

Rodney Fuentebella keyframe.

Leipzig, Germany. The sun is beginning to slide toward the horizon as Captain America and his team stands face-to-face with Tony Stark and his team. This moment—appropriately dubbed by the filmmakers the "splash panel" fight, due to its resemblance to a double-page comic-book spread—was the one the entire crew had been waiting for. "It was a pretty special day when you see the caliber of actors and these characters that you've cared about for years come together all in one place and sort of rush at each other," Executive Producer Nate Moore says. "There's an energy in the air that everybody in the crew felt—from the cameramen to the craft-service people to the stunt people."

Marvel Co-President and Executive Producer Louis D'Esposito adds, "There's something really magical about seeing these characters from all different franchises come together and be in the same space. It's something that we could never sort of imagine. You write it on the page, you talk about it in meetings, and it seems really smart and really interesting—but when you see it in person, there's something that is really mind-blowing about it."

Bringing this magical moment to the screen wasn't an easy task. "We spent months pre-visualizing the fight, basically going into the computer and planning the attack," Visual Effects Supervisor Dan Deleeuw says. "One of the biggest complications about a scene like this is the sheer number of heroes we have fighting each other. So when we're on set, we'll actually take a look at the pre-vis as we shoot—our heroes will fight to the plan we created months and months before."

SCOTT LANG / ANT-MAN

While he's not yet a heavy hitter next to figures like the Hulk, Ant-Man's skill set represents an undeniable asset to Captain America's team. Lead Visual Development Concept Illustrator Andy Park, who designed the original Ant-Man suit, was tasked with the character's redesign for Marvel's *Captain America: Civil War*. "I loved designing the Ant-Man suit for the *Ant-Man* film, and am very proud of its overall look and how it came out in the film," Park says. "I felt like it was very successful in its resolve and design.

Andy Park concept art.

"Of course, the suit for the *Ant-Man* film was designed that way because it had to look like it was created in the '60s by Hank Pym—it had to have a retro feel to it. *Civil War* was our opportunity to update the suit. The challenge was how to update it without taking away the elements that made the original Ant-Man suit cool and unique. So in designing the look, I tried to keep the same overall feel. I didn't want to create a suit that felt like too obvious a departure from his original look. On second glance, you will see that it's slicker and more modern. It's less clunky, overall, and yet I tried to keep elements such as exposed tubing throughout the suit. In all reality, a modern suit probably wouldn't have exposed tubing as much as we have it, but I realized that it is part of the charm of the suit.

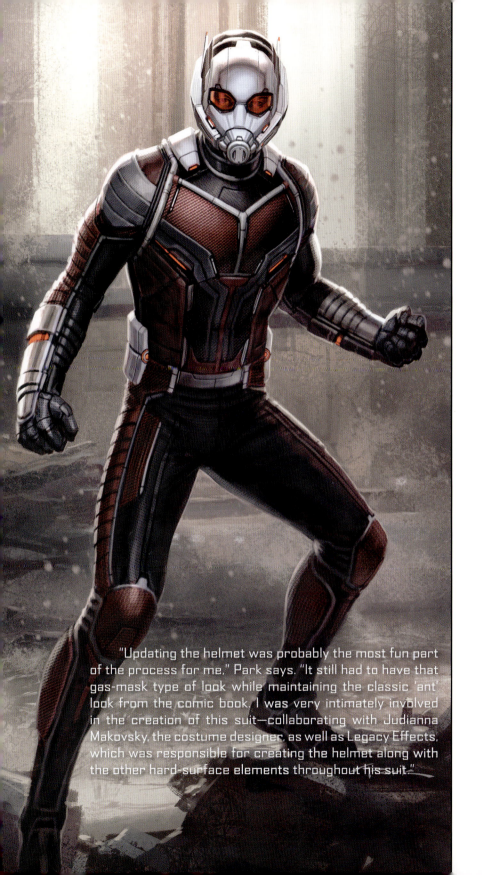

"Updating the helmet was probably the most fun part of the process for me," Park says. "It still had to have that gas-mask type of look while maintaining the classic 'ant' look from the comic book. I was very intimately involved in the creation of this suit—collaborating with Judianna Makovsky, the costume designer, as well as Legacy Effects, which was responsible for creating the helmet along with the other hard-surface elements throughout his suit."

CHAPTER FIVE: CIVIL WAR

Andy Park concept art.

CLINT BARTON / HAWKEYE

Clint Barton called it quits at the end of Marvel's *Avengers: Age of Ultron*, but his retirement was short-lived. In a departure from his typical look, Hawkeye enters the fray with a streamlined, tactical uniform that still sports a few subtle nods to his comic-book appearance. "Much like Black Widow, Hawkeye's design changes are not overhauls by any means," Andy Park says. "His change in looks really reflects the specific story in mind, along with the tastes of the directors. The Russo brothers do have a sensibility that lends to a more grounded spin to their classic comic-book roots.

Andy Park concept art.

"Hawkeye's look in our cinematic universe, which was inspired by Bryan Hitch's design from *The Ultimates* comic book, has always had a more utilitarian take than the very purple costume and mask he donned in the other comic books." Park says. "I did want to try and inject the iconic purple in places with this concept. It's very minimal, but still adds a certain uniqueness and character to the overall look. I also implemented asymmetry with his sleeves as a nod to an early version of Hawkeye in the comics."

CHAPTER FIVE: CIVIL WAR

RIGHT FACING

Andy Park concept art.

John Eaves concept art.

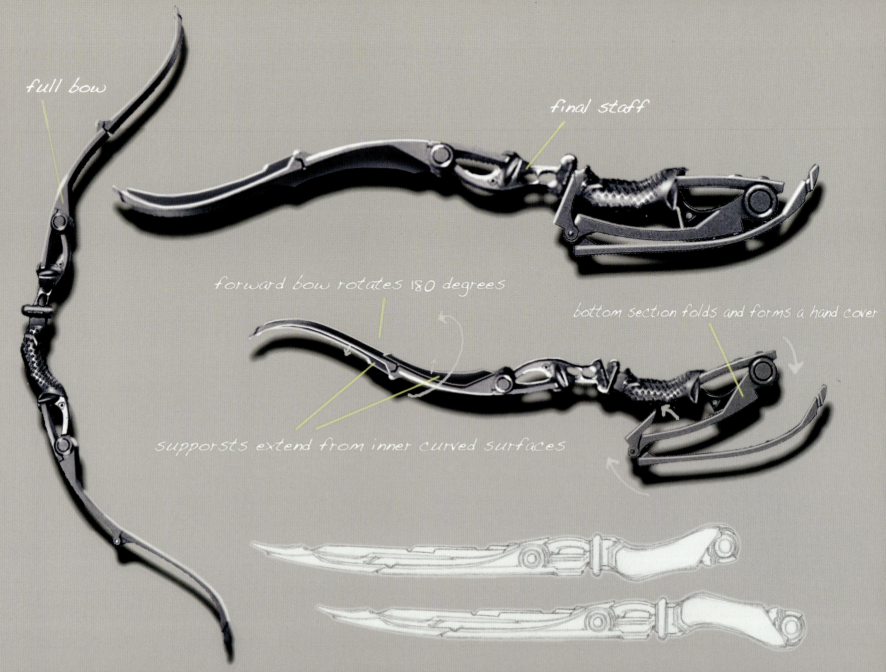

full bow

final staff

forward bow rotates 180 degrees

bottom section folds and forms a hand cover

supporsts extend from inner curved surfaces

Hawkeye's bow has been upgraded for each of the master marksman's cinematic appearances, and Marvel's *Captain America: Civil War* is no exception. "What you're seeing here is the third version of Hawkeye's bow, and we've added in a few new surprises, made a few changes," Property Master Russell Bobbitt says. "It's lightweight and easy to handle, and—because Jeremy Renner is a lefty—we made it left-handed. Overall, it's the same basic design except slicker and thinner—a bit more streamlined all the way around. For the quiver, we went back to the design from *Marvel's The Avengers* with a few general modifications."

John Eaves concept art.

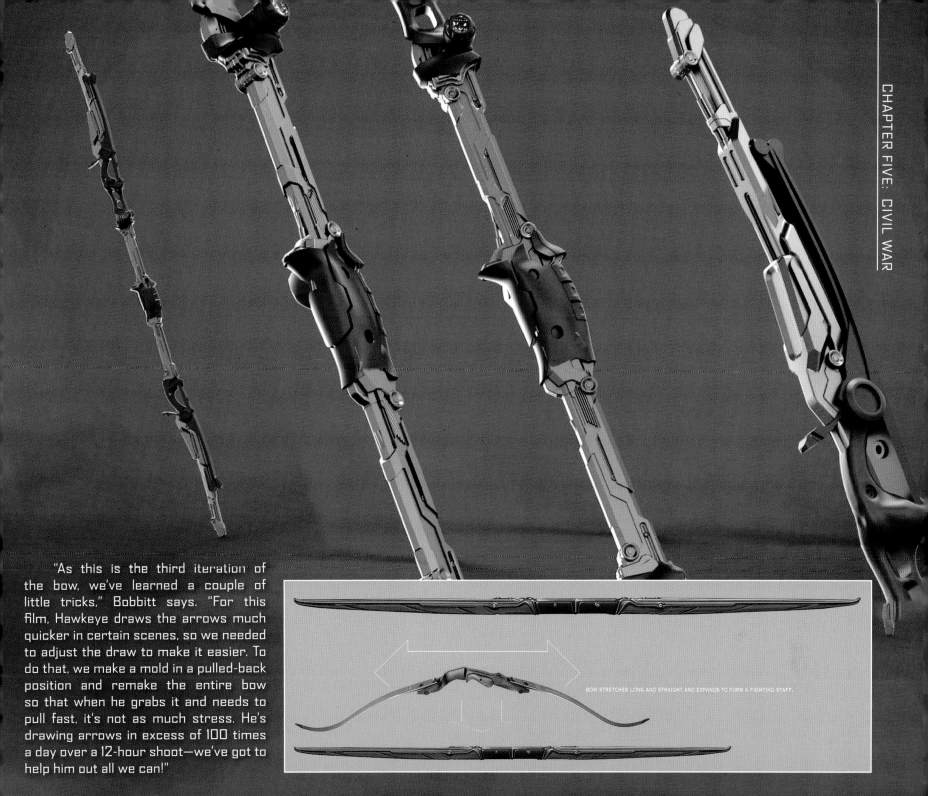

CHAPTER FIVE: CIVIL WAR

"As this is the third iteration of the bow, we've learned a couple of little tricks," Bobbitt says. "For this film, Hawkeye draws the arrows much quicker in certain scenes, so we needed to adjust the draw to make it easier. To do that, we make a mold in a pulled-back position and remake the entire bow so that when he grabs it and needs to pull fast, it's not as much stress. He's drawing arrows in excess of 100 times a day over a 12-hour shoot—we've got to help him out all we can!"

BOW STRETCHES LONG AND STRAIGHT AND EXPANDS TO FORM A FIGHTING STAFF.

John Eaves concept art.

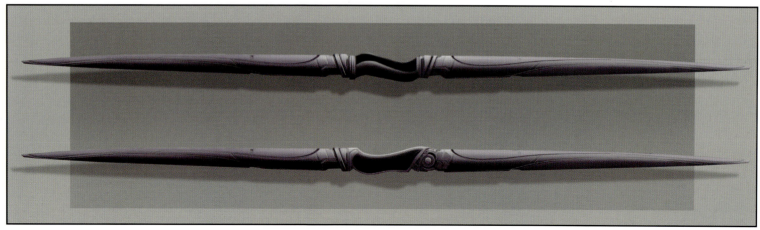

John Eaves concept art.

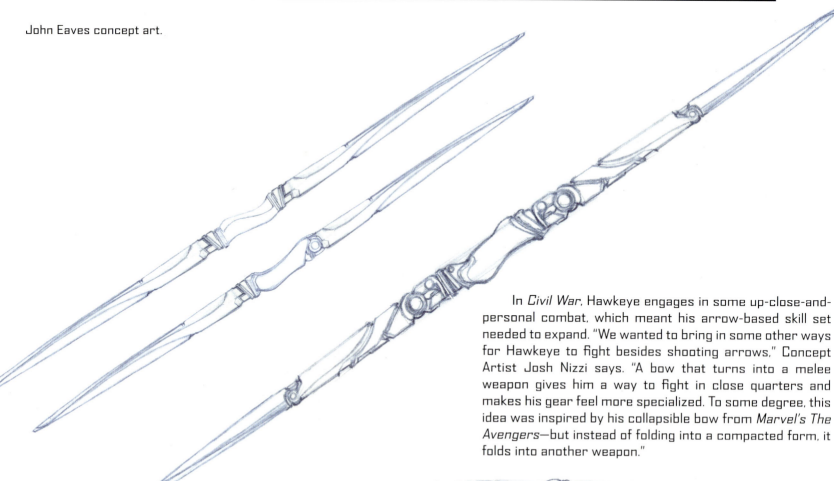

In *Civil War*, Hawkeye engages in some up-close-and-personal combat, which meant his arrow-based skill set needed to expand. "We wanted to bring in some other ways for Hawkeye to fight besides shooting arrows," Concept Artist Josh Nizzi says. "A bow that turns into a melee weapon gives him a way to fight in close quarters and makes his gear feel more specialized. To some degree, this idea was inspired by his collapsible bow from *Marvel's The Avengers*—but instead of folding into a compacted form, it folds into another weapon."

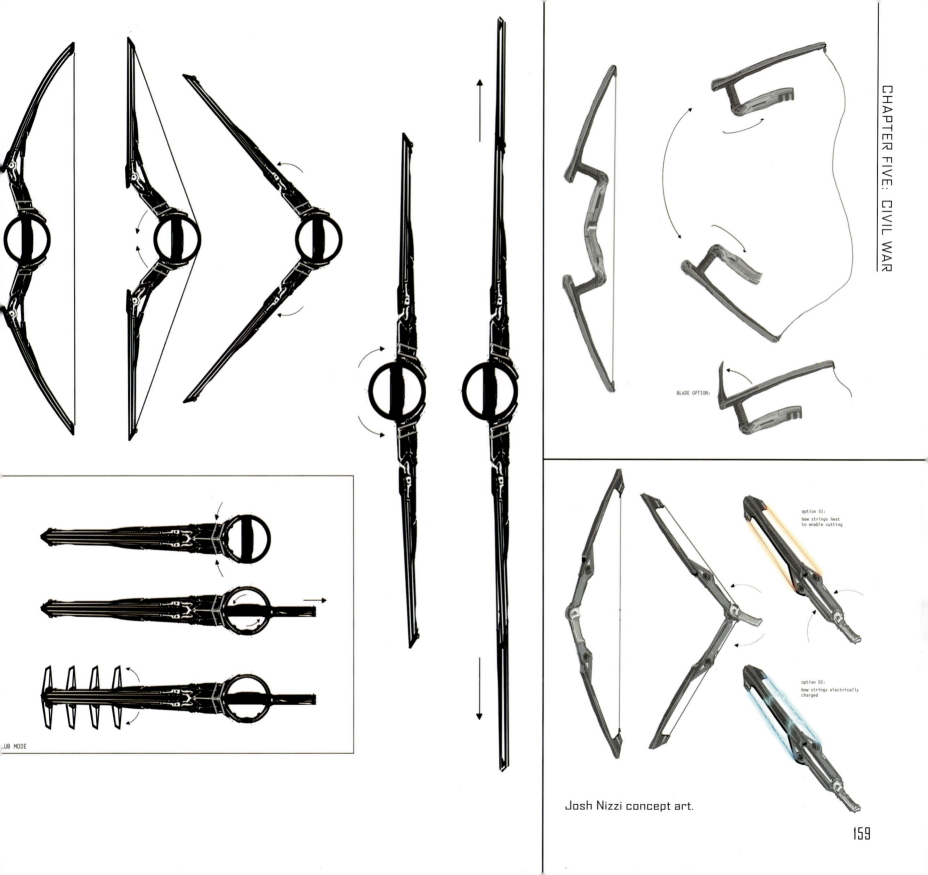

CHAPTER FIVE: CIVIL WAR

Josh Nizzi concept art.

Josh Nizzi concept art.   Josh Nizzi concept art.

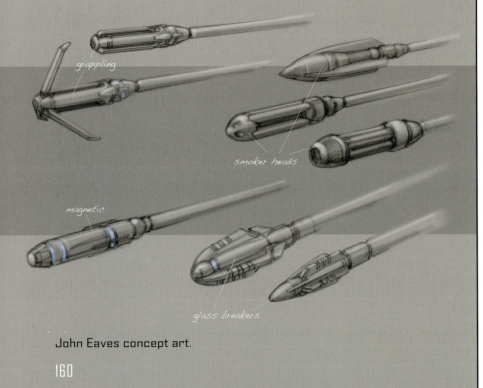

John Eaves concept art.

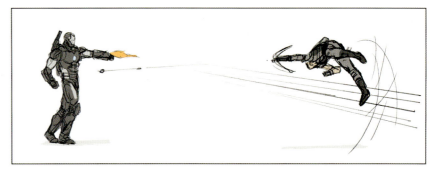

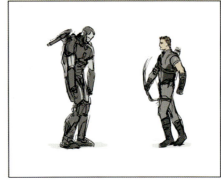

"I tried to come up with arrow tips that would be specifically geared toward fighting against Iron Man or War Machine," Nizzi says. "Since those characters rely on electrical power to operate, an obvious weakness would be an EMP arrow tip that could shut down their suits when activated. In order to combat against enemies in flight, a flack arrow would burst into a cloud of mini explosives that would do damage as well as disorient."

Josh Nizzi concept art.

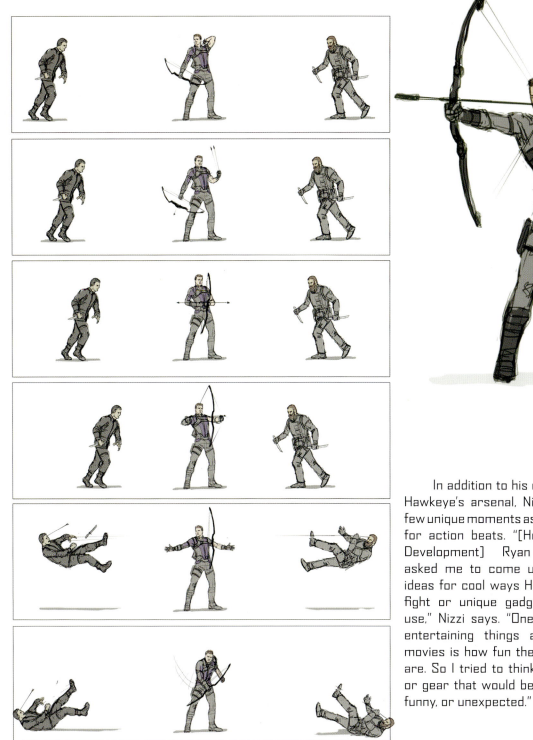

CHAPTER FIVE: CIVIL WAR

In addition to his exploration of Hawkeye's arsenal, Nizzi crafted a few unique moments as early options for action beats. "[Head of Visual Development] Ryan Meinerding asked me to come up with some ideas for cool ways Hawkeye could fight or unique gadgets he could use," Nizzi says. "One of the most entertaining things about Marvel movies is how fun the fight scenes are. So I tried to think of moments or gear that would be entertaining, funny, or unexpected."

Josh Nizzi concept art.

TONY STARK / IRON MAN

Iron Man's armor becomes sleeker and more polished with each upgrade. The design's smooth, linear shape and accents—and with this new iteration, an abundance of arc reactors—offer a glimpse into the genius mind of Tony Stark. "With a lot of the Iron Man suits, we've always tried to be inspired by suits that have appeared in the comics before, whether aesthetically or conceptually," Concept Artist Phil Saunders says. "One of the ones people had been eager for us to tackle was the comics' Bleeding Edge armor—even if this suit doesn't have the functionality of the Bleeding Edge armor. In *Iron Man 3*, we designed the Mark 42 with a level of detail complexity because of the

Phil Saunders concept art.

panel-attachment function—various plates flying onto him—which required a very fine line breakup. We were assuming that was going to be the way he continues to suit up. For both aesthetic and functional reasons, we felt it was necessary to continue that level of complexity in the Mark 45 armor, the last suit seen in *Avengers: Age of Ultron*. That suit was very organic with anatomical musculature. For this suit, the Mark 46, I wanted to take it back a little bit more toward a mechanical design while still keeping that level of musculature to it. You'll see in this design a lot of the lines flow more directly, and it has a much simpler color breakup."

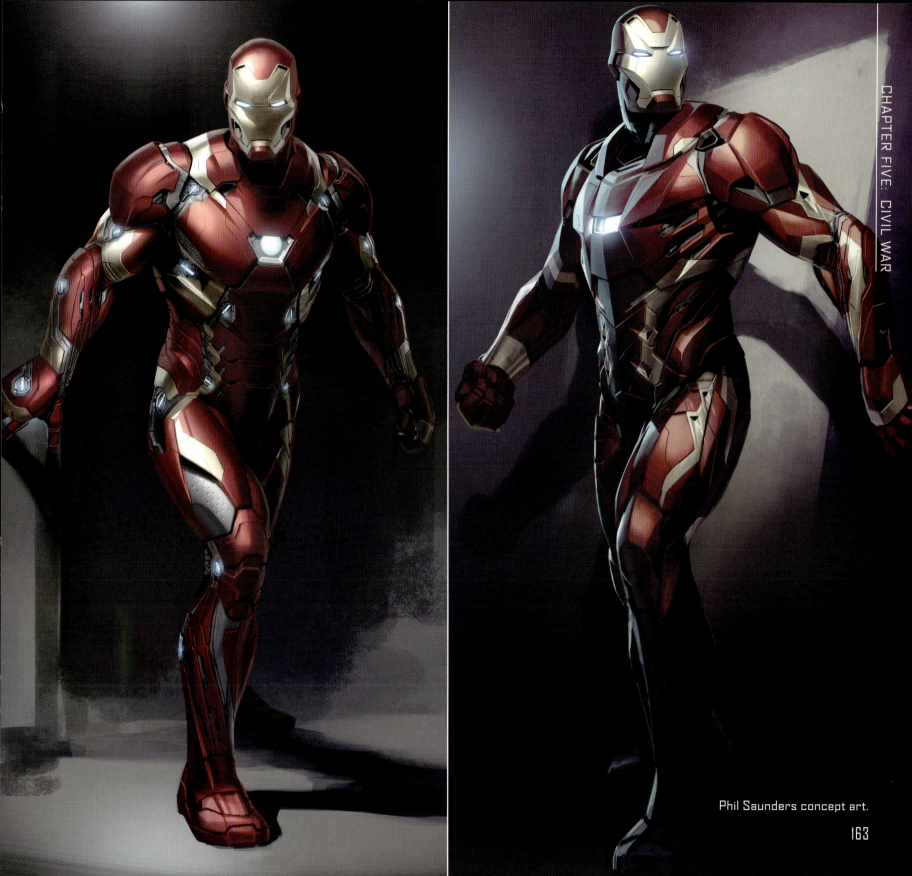

CHAPTER FIVE: CIVIL WAR

Phil Saunders concept art.

"Early on, there was going to be a stealth component to the suit," Saunders says. "We played around with a lot of different ideas on how that would work. Would it be some sort of mimetic surface texture that picks up light around it and changes color? Or the kind of projection system that's used on the Helicarrier, where you've got light-emitting panels? One of the thoughts I had was to use a number of projectors around the body that effectively would scan the environment around it, and then create an image of what's behind the suit. Hence the little lit RT projectors all over the body—those would light up and scan the environment, and project the environment onto the suit."

Phil Saunders concept art.

Josh Nizzi concept art.

Phil Saunders concept art.

CHAPTER FIVE: CIVIL WAR

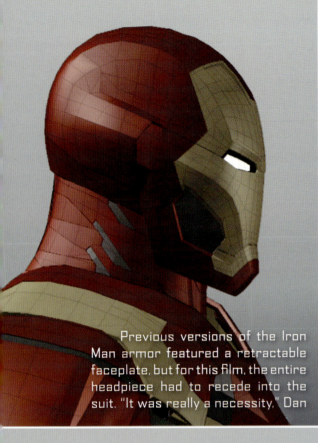
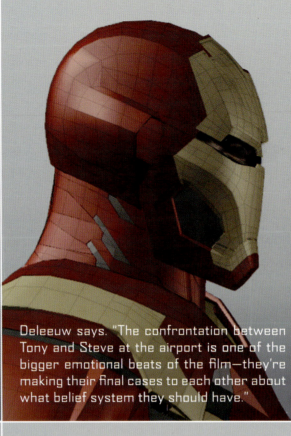

Previous versions of the Iron Man armor featured a retractable faceplate, but for this film, the entire headpiece had to recede into the suit. "It was really a necessity," Dan Deleeuw says. "The confrontation between Tony and Steve at the airport is one of the bigger emotional beats of the film—they're making their final cases to each other about what belief system they should have."

Andy Park concept art.

"Our executive producer, Nate Moore, mentioned that if Robert Downey Jr. had to deliver the lines with the helmet on and the visor up, it could pull back on his performance. Riffing on Star-Lord from *Guardians of the Galaxy*, the idea was that the helmet could break apart and go into the back of the suit. This notion was also building upon the idea established in *Iron Man 3* where the suit could break into component pieces," Deleeuw says.

CHAPTER FIVE: CIVIL WAR

AVENGERS VS. AVENGERS

Even before the lineups for Captain America and Iron Man's sides were finalized, the Visual Development team had begun conceptualizing moments of these iconic characters going head-to-head. The art was key to deciding not only the team alignments, but also the settings and orientation of the battles.

Andy Park keyframe.

"Very often when we illustrate our keyframes the script is not finalized yet," Andy Park says. "Therefore, we often get to illustrate moments that you'll never get to see in the final film. But the joy of coming up with these is actualizing what the moment could look like. It helps everyone in the filmmaking process visualize what is written on paper. Many of the keyframes I did were made when the teams were a bit different. For instance, Ant-Man/Giant-Man was on Team Stark in the early drafts."

Andy Park keyframe.

CHAPTER FIVE: CIVIL WAR

"When we were building the story of *Civil War*, we always knew this climatic battle was going to be important," Nate Moore says. "As storytellers, you start to try and figure out what's the best place for that to happen. Airports are interesting because they are very populated, but there are also isolated pockets to them. Also, if I were to tell you I needed to get myself and five other people somewhere very quickly, an airport seems like a good place to do it. Rather than an abandoned amusement park, which was something we considered early on, or a warehouse district, which feels very 'movie'—what's something that the audience hasn't really seen before, but also tells the story that these guys are on the run?"

"Once we decided narratively that that's what the story asked for, we started to look at different airports for various architectural elements that we found interesting," Moore says. "The Leipzig/Halle Airport has a terminal with these rounded glass windows and this interesting metal scaffolding around them that we found architecturally kind of fascinating."

Andy Park keyframe.

CHAPTER FIVE: CIVIL WAR

When the time came to finalize the teams, the filmmakers searched for an alignment that would match MCU history while maintaining excitement. "It was an extremely complicated process," Director Anthony Russo says. "We sat in a room for months and months with writers Chris Markus and Stephen McFeely, and Nate Moore, and we would come up with different scenarios. For us, it's all about character. It became about how do you combine character? Who are two people who are good to put in conflict with each other? Who are two people who have to make an easy alliance with one another? It was really just playing with all the fun and the combinations of those in the movie, and then figuring out how it fell out. There wasn't really a formula we used other than that we wanted to surprise ourselves and figure out what was fresh and new in the storytelling."

Rodney Fuentebella keyframe.

CHAPTER FIVE: CIVIL WAR

"We tracked where they've been in the MCU up to this point," Director Joe Russo says. "We talked about every possible choice that they could make. You want to surprise the audience. You want to make some choices that are interesting. If everyone can predict who's going to be on whose side going into the movie, we didn't do our job right. There are some surprising choices made in the film—choices that are all sort of substantiated on prior points of view that these characters have expressed in the MCU up to this point."

175

Andy Park keyframe.

CHAPTER FIVE: CIVIL WAR

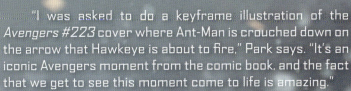

"I was asked to do a keyframe illustration of the *Avengers #223* cover where Ant-Man is crouched down on the arrow that Hawkeye is about to fire," Park says. "It's an iconic Avengers moment from the comic book, and the fact that we get to see this moment come to life is amazing."

"I would say what was really determinant, too, was that every single character had a personal, emotional reason for making the choice that they made," Anthony Russo says. "And that was trackable in their arc from the beginning to the end of the movie. The most fun part of deciding who sided where was figuring out what on the deepest level could move these characters to go one way or the other."

177

During the fight, Ant-Man penetrates Iron Man's suit—allowing him to take down Tony from the inside out. "I think people underestimate Ant-Man and what he's really capable of," Concept Artist Jackson Sze says. "We saw him fight Falcon back in the *Ant-Man* film when he was still learning to use his suit, and now we assume he's had even more time to hone his skills and really learn to fight creatively. He proves in this movie that he can hold his own with just about any Avenger."

Jackson Sze keyframes.

"Ant-Man has a history of being anti-Stark—a sentiment expressed by Hank Pym, who gives Scott Lang the suit in *Ant-Man*," Joe Russo says. "So he would naturally fall into that camp of being anti-Stark and anti-authority, as you can see also historically: As a criminal, he committed an anti-establishment crime to try and right some wrongs. He lines up pretty cleanly on Cap's side."

Jackson Sze keyframes.

Spider-Man's introduction into the Marvel Cinematic Universe was an exciting addition late in the development process. His appearance not only expands Marvel Studios' ever-growing roster of heroes, but helps balance the conflicting teams. As a character, Spider-Man has often been depicted as an agile teenager with lightning reflexes, traits Nate Moore says came as a package deal with the casting of Tom Holland. "When you see him on screen—especially next to characters like Tony Stark and Steve Rogers—he brings something special and different to that role because there is an innocence to him that's partially realized by the fact that Tom Holland is himself just a teenager," Moore says. "At the same time, we wanted Spider-Man to move unlike any Spider-Man in the other previous films. And Tom—having learned sort of theater acting and acrobatics by doing *Billy Elliot* in London—brings a natural physicality to the role that we were kind of surprised by. I mean, here's a kid who can do a standing backflip. That really helps when you're building action around the character, because you're not as dependent on stunt guys to breathe life into this character when he has the mask on. And I think actors inhabit part of the roles physically. So Tom was able to bring that physicality to the character of Spider-Man even when he had the mask on."

Rodney Fuentebella keyframe.

CHAPTER FIVE: CIVIL WAR

Josh Nizzi keyframe.

CHAPTER FIVE: CIVIL WAR

Josh Nizzi keyframe.

Along with the personalities, the filmmakers needed to balance the heroes' power sets for the strongest visual and emotional impact. "Rhodey is Tony's oldest and closest friend," says Executive Producer and Head of Physical Production Victoria Alonso. "He comes from a military background and understands structure and order; he understands discipline and a need for oversight. It's clear why he joins Tony's team. He was the perfect person to pit against Falcon, who is Cap's brother-in-arms, his best friend in the modern world. They're aerial masters, and they elevate the fight to a playing field outside of the tarmac."

When the situation becomes dire for Cap's team, Ant-Man takes the battle to new heights—literally. Bringing Giant-Man to life was all about finding the right tactic. Dan Deleeuw says. "There's all these classic B-movies from the '50s where they used oversized people and over-cranked the camera, then played it back so it felt slo-mo. It's neat, but it doesn't always work. We did experiment with shooting Paul Rudd over-cranked, and then used that performance to match the digital animation we did. We decided to go full CG because it allowed us to control more of his movements and so much of the detail in the costume."

Andy Park keyframe.

CHAPTER FIVE: CIVIL WAR

"Shooting in an airport, we also had a lot of great scale reference—cars, tugs, luggage—for more of the normal-sized heroes, and then you've got jets that Giant-Man can be standing next to or falling into or even tearing wings off of to use as weapons," Deleeuw says. "We started looking at this sequence early on in pre-viz, where the original idea was to ramp up his size progressively during the fight. So he'd start at 15 feet, and then grow to another size, and then finally to the massive version we see in the film. It was cool, but it also kind of defeated the reveal—so we decided to save the moment for the middle of the fight and go straight to 50-foot-tall."

187

"There's a natural youthful clumsiness to Tom that's endearing and becomes so much part of his performance that it integrated uniquely into the typical Spidey acrobatics," Deleeuw says. "During the visual-effects process, it was all about mechanics. He can't just swing through the air and not have the mechanics of what the body needs to do to propel him through the air. I think what you'll find—even though we do hit the iconic 'Spidey poses'—is that the in-betweens are not as fluid or as graceful. His body struggles to put him into those positions, and it's a function of it being his first time out. He's still figuring it all out and coming into himself."

"The Russo brothers wanted to stay grounded, but still convey that true comic-book feel," Visual Effects Producer Jen Underdahl says. "When you see him on screen, it's him. It's Spider-Man like we've never seen him before. He elevates the scenes in a really fun way."

Andy Park keyframe.

CHAPTER FIVE: CIVIL WAR

Andy Park keyframe.

"It was already iconic having most of the Avengers characters squaring off with the additions of the Winter Soldier, Ant-Man, and Black Panther," Park says. "But once Spider-Man joined the fray, it was a lineup of characters that many fans never thought they'd see together. It is truly a special moment in the Marvel Cinematic Universe to have arguably the most recognizable character in all of comic books join the party."

CHAPTER FIVE: CIVIL WAR

Andy Park keyframe.

193

Rodney Fuentebella keyframe.

CHAPTER FIVE: CIVIL WAR

THE RAFT

Following the events at the airport, our bruised and beaten heroes are remanded to a state-of-the-art underwater prison. "In the comics, there was a similar prison on a cliffside overlooking the water," Production Designer Owen Paterson says. "However, the filmmakers were keen on creating something that was far more isolated. We came up with this idea that it would be self-contained—a bit like a submarine in the sense that it could rise up to the surface cloaked, uncloak itself for a helicopter or plane to land, and then submerge itself down below the water."

John Eaves concept art.

CHAPTER FIVE: CIVIL WAR

"For the shape, we started with a bolt—which had a really cool shape of cast metal, very heavily built steel and titanium. We said, 'Okay, this isn't like a submarine that travels the world—it's more like a submarine building,'" Paterson says. "We also looked at some really interesting-looking forts that were built off the English coast in the Second World War—they're concrete and kind of round with a flat top. They sit in the water and reach all the way to the bottom, while this structure could actually rise and fall."

John Eaves concept art.

Andrew Leung concept art.

CHAPTER FIVE: CIVIL WAR

Andrew Leung concept art.

199

Andrew Leung concept art.

Andrew Leung concept art.

CHAPTER FIVE: CIVIL WAR

201

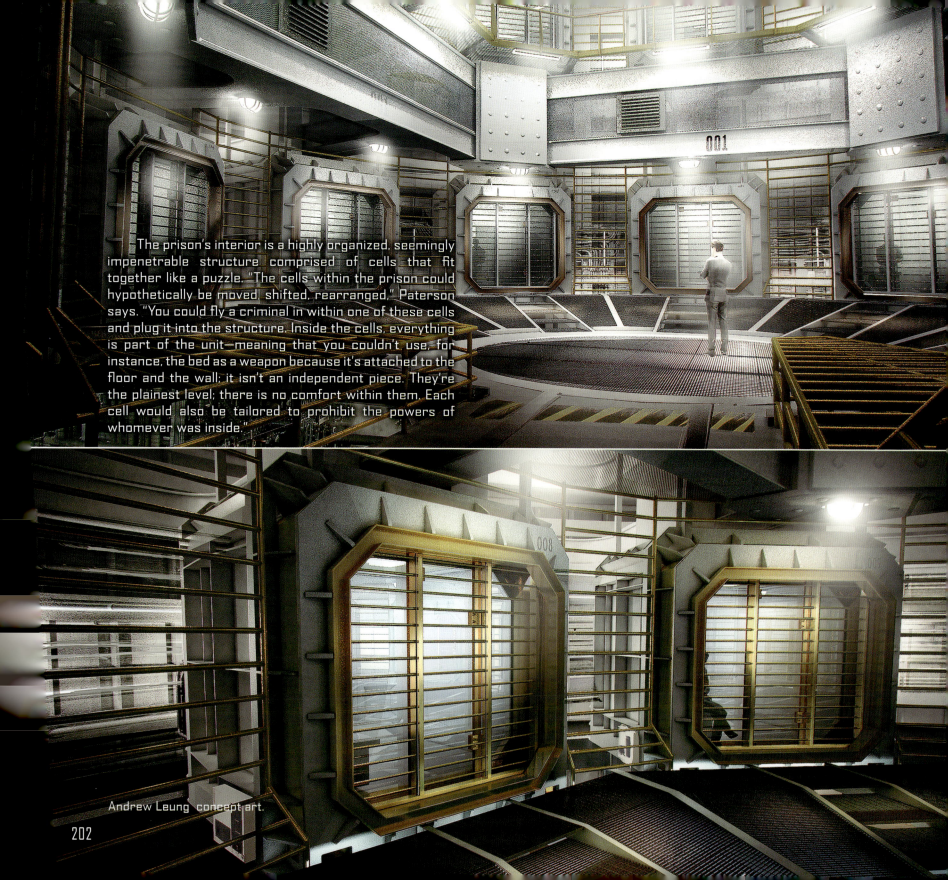

The prison's interior is a highly organized, seemingly impenetrable structure comprised of cells that fit together like a puzzle. "The cells within the prison could hypothetically be moved, shifted, rearranged," Paterson says. "You could fly a criminal in within one of these cells and plug it into the structure. Inside the cells, everything is part of the unit—meaning that you couldn't use, for instance, the bed as a weapon because it's attached to the floor and the wall; it isn't an independent piece. They're the plainest level; there is no comfort within them. Each cell would also be tailored to prohibit the powers of whomever was inside."

Andrew Leung concept art.

"Originally we looked at using orange jumpsuits for the prisoners, but felt they seemed a bit too similar to the yellow prison outfits seen in the Kyln in *Guardians of the Galaxy*," says Producer and President of Marvel Studios Kevin Feige. "Instead, we chose to go with a darker blue, which was aesthetically quite different from the uniforms in the Kyln."

Mariano Diaz concept art.

Andres Cubillan concept art.

CHAPTER FIVE: CIVIL WAR

CHAPTER SIX
ORIGINAL SINS

The snow falls against a dreary tundra outside a monolithic underground base, foreshadowing a somber finale. The shot's stripped-down pathos brings audiences close to the film's centerpiece characters, the heart of the Avengers: Iron Man and Captain America. After learning the true identity of the man behind the UN bombing and obtaining Steve Rogers and Bucky Barnes' location from Falcon, Tony Stark takes off in pursuit. Apprehensive, but knowing his actions benefit the greater good, Tony joins forces with Captain America and Bucky on their mission to put an end to Zemo's plan to revive a group of super-soldiers just as powerful as the Winter Soldier. Putting aside their differences over the Sokovia Accords, the massive brawl in Germany, and their opposing ideologies on leadership, Stark, Rogers, and Barnes set forth into the dark tunnels to put an end to the villain inside. It isn't long before the trio realizes the true threat is something more sinister than any villain we've seen in the Marvel Cinematic Universe thus far. "It's a ruse—Zemo has played them from the start, manipulating them emotionally and psychologically," Executive Producer and Head of Physical Production Victoria Alonso says. "It goes deeper than that, too. Deeper and darker, revealing things that go back to the beginning of the Marvel Cinematic Universe, which is always very interesting to explore."

As the truth comes tumbling out, Stark and Rogers once again find themselves at odds—and this time, they won't be pulling punches. "It's a gritty, gut-wrenching finale," Alonso continues. "We've followed these characters for so long, celebrating their successes, lamenting their failures—and now we're being forced to watch them tear each other apart. It's poignant, layered storytelling."

Ryan Meinerding keyframe.

HYDRA BASE

The setting of the film—a desolate region of Siberia—borrowed an unused concept from a previous entry in the series, according to Visual Effects Supervisor Dan Deleeuw. "There was some artwork done back on Marvel's *Captain America: The Winter Soldier* where we actually saw where he was created, where he was stored when he wasn't out on missions," Deleeuw says of the Winter Soldier's origins. "That sequence ultimately ended up being cut, but we always liked the idea. It fits his history, if you remember back to *Captain America: The First Avenger* where Bucky falls off the mountain train and down into a snowy ravine. Everything that revolves around Bucky has this somber, cold-winter feel. It's what drove us to this location."

Maciej Kuciara keyframe.

CHAPTER SIX: ORIGINAL SINS

"Building on that was: Where was the exact location we wanted to place him? We thought maybe the North Sea at first, and maybe there's some submarine pens near an abandoned Russian base," Deleeuw says. "And from there it became about various types of Russian bases, where we finally landed on using an abandoned missile silo that Hydra had come in and taken control of. To achieve this, we actually captured plates from Iceland, because we knew we were going to be shooting the bulk of the film in Atlanta. We built a partial snow set outside and replaced the background with the plates from Iceland."

"We did a digital 360 on Google Maps of a place called Hafursey in Iceland," Visual Effects Producer Jen Underdahl says. "We sent a helicopter out there to shoot it, and it was absolutely gorgeous. It was super snowy with a beautiful clear-blue sky; it was absolutely stunning. Two weeks later, we sent another unit out there, and the snow was melting. It was almost gone; it was super cloudy and grim. It was not at all what we had originally shown the Russo brothers as footage that we were going to shoot, but they loved it even more. They thought, 'This is it—this is Zemo's final moment.' The tone of the environment really acted as a metaphor to his character. It was all serendipitous."

Maciej Kuciara keyframe.

CHAPTER SIX: ORIGINAL SINS

Maciej Kuciara keyframe.

The characters' descent into the subterranean Hydra base proves to be a transformative experience for all involved. "The darkness accentuates the heroes in a haunting way," says Victoria Alonso. "We're putting Iron Man in an environment where he can't really freely fly around. There's restrictions to his movement, and it allows for a more personal interaction among the other characters."

CHAPTER SIX: ORIGINAL SINS

"When these ballistic-missile bases were first built in the '50s or '60s, there was fresh concrete and fresh paint, and they probably looked a bit more inviting than the version we see in the film," Alonso says. "Obviously, 50-plus years have gone by, Hydra had been using it to breed and train super-soldiers, and now it's a rundown, grungy shell."

Maciej Kuciara keyframe.

CHAPTER SIX: ORIGINAL SINS

STASIS CHAMBER

Ryan Meinerding concept art.

"Architecturally, there are a lot of cylindrical shapes we felt mirrored the stasis pod that Bucky was kept in. There's sort of a macro design element that these micro pods sit in very comfortably," says Executive Producer Nate Moore. "So in essence, the room itself is a giant stasis pod in which there are six smaller stasis pods. It makes for a really interesting design element."

Rodney Fuentebella concept art.

"There's a lot of atmosphere in the stasis chamber, with the effects of dry ice and digital enhancement," Victoria Alonso says. "It created an even more mysterious and visceral environment. It's a journey of discovery for all of the characters at this point—they're trying to find Zemo and stop him from unleashing the super-soldiers, while at the same time learning things about the past, especially for Bucky."

CHAPTER SIX — ORIGINAL SINS

Designed to feel like elevated tech, the stasis pods nonetheless needed to maintain a dated aesthetic, having been built 30 years prior. "We gathered a lot of reference for the stasis pods, and our main goal was to fabricate a chair that could fit into a cylinder in a very specific way," Production Designer Owen Paterson says. "We put it onto a half-cog so it could move as the cylinder around it opened up. You look at it and see that it feels very heavy—that it's made with cast-iron machine pieces that offer a very complex aesthetic, while also feeling a bit rudimentary like you could buy it at a hardware store."

Rodney Fuentebella concept art.

CHAPTER SIX: ORIGINAL SINS

"By adding in the atmosphere, you get the idea that it's a cryo facility—that these people are frozen in stasis," Paterson says. "There's also an excess amount of grime that's built up over the years while these people have been stuck, waiting. If no one had stumbled down here, these super-soldiers could have been frozen for another 20 or 30 or 50 years. It is really a unique space, though—there's a real gravitas to the pods and the chamber they're kept in."

CHAPTER SIX: ORIGINAL SINS

Paul Ozzimo concept art.

David Moreau concept art.

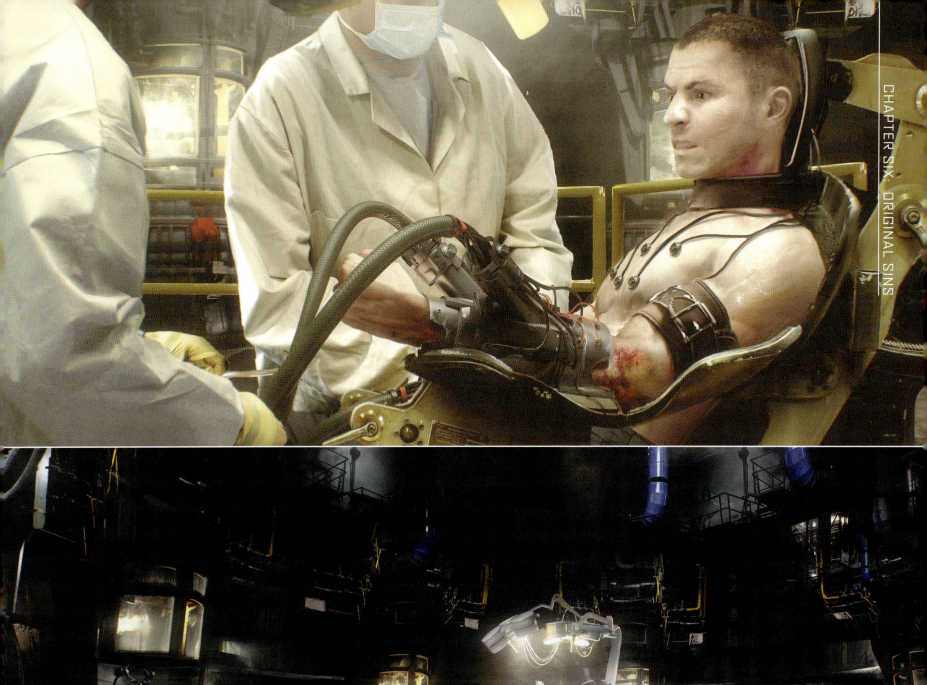

CHAPTER SIX. ORIGINAL SINS

Maciej Kuciara keyframe.

SUPER-SOLDIER PROGRAM

Injected with the same serum as Bucky, the super-soldiers stored in the Hydra facility played a much larger role early in the film's development—and consequently required a wave of conceptualization. "Their looks needed to be simple; everything about their look was emphasizing their strength and ferocity," Costume Designer Judianna Makovsky says. "Keeping the garment close to their body would allow for easier movement with fighting hand-to-hand, much like training gear—it wouldn't impede movement, and it would be extremely action-friendly."

Mariano Diaz concept art.

Christian Cordella concept art.

Christian Cordella concept art.

CHAPTER SIX: ORIGINAL SINS

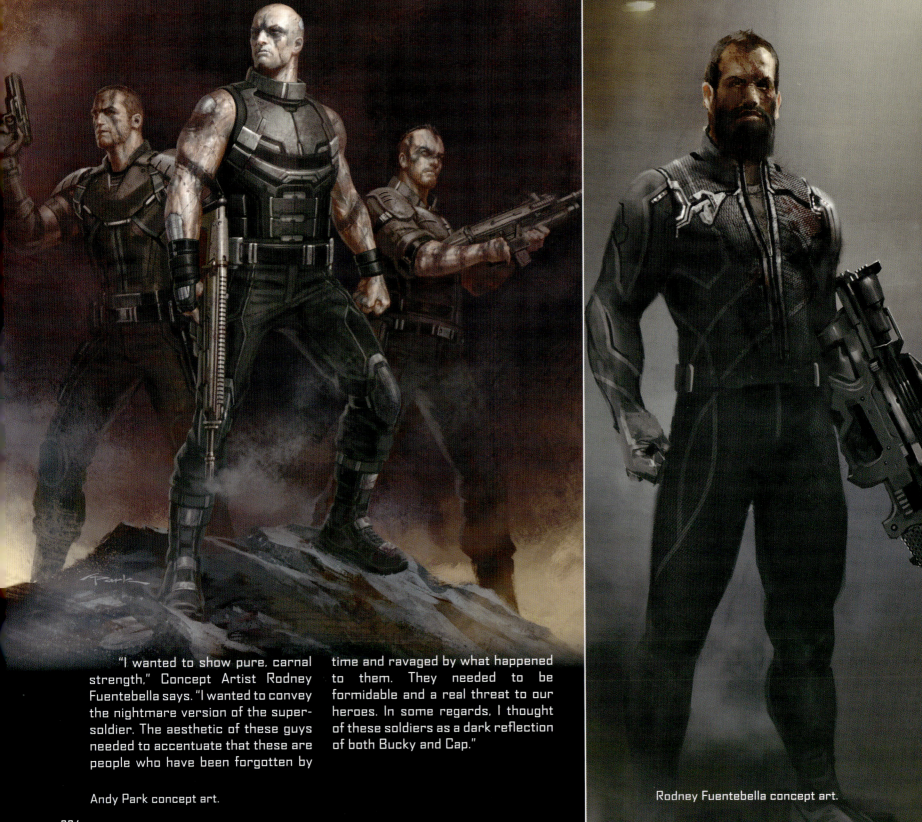

"I wanted to show pure, carnal strength," Concept Artist Rodney Fuentebella says. "I wanted to convey the nightmare version of the super-soldier. The aesthetic of these guys needed to accentuate that these are people who have been forgotten by time and ravaged by what happened to them. They needed to be formidable and a real threat to our heroes. In some regards, I thought of these soldiers as a dark reflection of both Bucky and Cap."

Andy Park concept art.

Rodney Fuentebella concept art.

CHAPTER SIX: ORIGINAL SINS

Josh Nizzi concept art.

Rodney Fuentebella concept art.

CHAPTER SIX: ORIGINAL SINS

Rodney Fuentebella concept art.

"The super-soldiers are all prisoners, and their cells mirror the mentality of the time period," Owen Paterson says. "It's simple, and tonally very dark and dank. It's very primitive, which conveys this primal aura that really fits the characters and the events."

CHAPTER SIX: ORIGINAL SINS

Manuel Plank-Jorge concept art.

Nathan Schroeder concept art

CHAPTER SIX: ORIGINAL SINS

Manuel Plank-Jorge concept art.

DECEMBER 16, 1991

"We saw an underground bunker that was commandeered by Hydra during *Captain America: The Winter Soldier*, so we really wanted to make sure we were offering a visually dynamic, different type of space for this one," Victoria Alonso says. "The combination of color here really sets it apart—the splashes of rust give the rooms a lot of texture and also history."

Marek Okon concept art.

CHAPTER SIX: ORIGINAL SINS

CHAPTER SIX: ORIGINAL SINS

"It's interesting when you have a character like Iron Man who can fly and shoot repulsor blasts," Nate Moore says. "If the rooms are too big, and he has too much room to move, it becomes a very uneven fight with Cap, who is somewhat ground-bound. That's why we push the fight into the missile silo—where there's really no place to fly, and Cap can get to him within a couple steps. It really leveled the playing field."

Maciej Kuciara concept art.

IRON MAN VS. CAP AND BUCKY

A series of revelations sends Iron Man over the edge and the final confrontation between Cap, Bucky, and Tony begins. "We always knew the battle in the third act was going to be very personal," Nate Moore says. "We also had to sell to the audience that it was going to be grand. Initially when you see the Hydra facility, you only see the stasis-pod chamber and the training center—really big open spaces so that when the audience sees the film they get the idea that the scope is going to be really big, and this is where the final fight will take place. We had a bigger idea, though, with what Zemo's plan actually was. So while we could start in those spacious areas, like the stasis chamber, we did want to force them into areas that became more and more confined. It had to come down to a hand-to-hand battle."

Maciej Kuciara concept art.

"The silo was also a doorway out into the world," Moore says. "We wanted in this sequence to give the idea that Bucky could escape. While he could have just run through a door back into the tundra, that's visually not too interesting. To see him try to climb out through the top of the missile silo as the hatch is opening was far more intriguing. Alternatively, it gives Iron Man a simple solution to stop him which is to blow the hatch. It narratively gives a moment in the fight for salvation—and then it's quickly taken away, and you're plunged back into the darkness of the space."

CHAPTER SIX: ORIGINAL SINS

Iron Man is relentless. His sarcasm has subsided, and he fights like a man possessed. "Part of what made the final battle so intriguing wasn't just that these were two huge icons fighting one another," Director Anthony Russo says. "They're both also, in a sense, leaders of the Avengers—Tony coming from his Stark point of view of 'I bring the money, and I bring the tech' and all that, and Cap from his sort of morally grounded point of view that gives him the right of leadership."

Maciej Kuciara concept art.

CHAPTER SIX: ORIGINAL SINS

Maciej Kuciara concept art.

CHAPTER SIX: ORIGINAL SINS

"What was great about the silo set was you could go from the main body—which was really cool, beautifully built, and aged—up to the very top of a missile silo, the middle of it, and the base," Owen Paterson says. "The fight there is very unique. I don't know if we've ever seen anything quite like it. It's very personal while also feeling visually compelling. It's this kind of strange environment like a tube with all this steel work in it; it also had some great elements. We played with the idea of, if a real rocket was taking off, you would have these vents that would go through the side of the hill where our set was located and blast out on the side. And though we never see that happen, it created a very nice piece of architecture for our film."

Ryan Meinerding keyframe.

Captain America actor Chris Evans attributes part of the character's evolution to his uncertainty. "What I think is nice about where they're pushing him is that it's the first time Steve doesn't really know the answer," Evans says. "I mean, in the first Captain America film, it's pretty clear that Hydra is bad. We can all agree with that. In *Captain America: The Winter Soldier*, S.H.I.E.L.D. is being run by Hydra. No conflict there. In the Avengers movies, aliens are no good—we want to fight them. It's always pretty cut-and-dried for him to know which side of the coin to fall on—it's why this film is tricky, because this conflict is a little more akin to day-to-day struggles that we all go through where there's no right and there's no wrong. I think it's hard for him to understand what the right thing to do is and what his role is."

CHAPTER SIX: ORIGINAL SINS

Andy Park keyframe.

Ryan Meinerding concept art.

"I have a great affinity for Tony Stark, and also for Steve Rogers," says Head of Visual Development Ryan Meinerding. "I've designed a number of looks for each throughout the evolution of the Marvel Cinematic Universe. Trying to read through the script and understand where the characters were meant to be, emotionally, was super important for me. I can see through both characters' eyes easily, especially with this story where things are a bit grayer. So to create a frame, usually you're meant to be very unambiguous and clear about the intention. It was extremely challenging to figure out the frames that would make sense. Any time I made Cap feel like he had the upper hand and Tony was on his last legs, it felt terrible—and the reverse for when Iron Man was 'winning.'"

Ryan Meinerding keyframe.

CHAPTER SIX: ORIGINAL SINS

"Since Cap is thought of as levelheaded, mostly in control, and the righteous man, putting him in a position where it feels like Tony is actually in danger as a result of Steve felt like the most compelling frames," Meinerding says. "Seeing that Tony is afraid of Steve in those moments was powerful. As an audience member, I don't think people expect Captain America to be pushed to the point where he would actually hurt Tony. In this story, you're taken to that edge with Steve—that's why those were the moments I ended up illustrating."

Ryan Meinerding keyframe.

CHAPTER SIX: ORIGINAL SINS

CHAPTER SEVEN
MARKETING CAPTAIN AMERICA: CIVIL WAR

Head of Visual Development Ryan Meinerding and Lead Visual Development Concept Illustrator Andy Park collaborated on a tryptic poster intended as a big reveal at the 2015 San Diego Comic-Con, as they'd done for prior Marvel films. "Before we decided to make three separate posters that you could fit together to make a single image, I did a series of other options that focused more on the fight between Captain America, Bucky, and Iron Man," Meinerding says. "The challenge with all of these was trying to keep a level of mystery, because at the time—we were just starting to shoot the movie—we definitely wanted to be careful with what we were going to show.

In the past, the posters were oftentimes used to be first reveals of the new looks for the heroes, so I started doing more team-centric concepts. Eventually there was one that seemed to stand out from the rest with the filmmakers, and we went down that path. I focused on two of the posters while Andy Park did the other. We weren't setting out to reveal the teams per se, but rather deliver an exciting, chaotic fight scene featuring all the characters—with Captain America and Iron Man clashing in the center." In the end, the filmmakers decided to save the posters for later in the marketing campaign.

Ryan Meinerding concept art.

EVEN: MARKETING CAPTAIN AMERICA: CIVIL WAR

Ryan Meinerding concept art.

CHAPTER SEVEN: MARKETING CAPTAIN AMERICA: CIVIL WAR

CHAPTER SEVEN: MARKETING CAPTAIN AMERICA: CIVIL WAR

Ant-Man, Hawkeye, Scarlet Witch, and Vision concept art by Andy Park; Black Widow, Captain America, Iron Man, Falcon, War Machine, Black Panther, and Winter Soldier concept art by Ryan Meinerding.

Andy Park
concept art.

Ryan Meinerding
concept art.

Ryan Meinerding
concept art.

Ryan Meinerding concept art.

AFTERWORD 2016

In the time I've spent at Marvel Studios, I've had the honor of working on some of the Marvel Universe's most iconic characters—most created over 50 years ago, and each with a multilayered history and definitive impact on popular culture. Helping bring them to the big screen is literally my dream job. Oftentimes, it's as overwhelming and stressful as it is rewarding, but the amazing experience of seeing characters I've loved all my life appear on screen—in a fully realized universe as big as it is in the comics—instantly transforms me from someone who worked on the movie to the fanboy I really am.

I've been fortunate enough to have worked on all of the films in both the Iron Man and Captain America trilogies. I love these characters and the journeys that the filmmakers have taken them on. *Captain America: Civil War* is truly a special journey because of the emotional weight that the conflict carries with it: Both Tony Stark and Steve Rogers have long histories in the Marvel Cinematic Universe, and seeing these friends torn apart is one of the most powerful stories Marvel Studios has told. Thank you Kevin, Joe, and Anthony for this amazing movie. All of us in the Visual Development team owe a tremendous debt to you for creating an incredible story, as well as for your direction and insight. Whatever quality and thoughtfulness exists in our designs is directly related to what you, Victoria, Louis, and Nate have brought to the material.

The Visual Development team that worked to translate the characters and moments from the comic-book page into the work displayed in this book is a tight-knit group of artists who collaborate, brainstorm, work and rework, pull all-nighters, agonize over details, and finally deliver some of the highest-quality concept art that is being made in film today. They do it because they love the characters as much as I do, and they love the universe that Kevin Feige and the rest of Marvel Studios has expertly constructed. I feel lucky to have worked with all of them, and owe them so much for their talent, dedication, hard work, and focus. Because of all the characters in this film, we relied heavily on many of the artists who had previously designed characters in the MCU. Phil Saunders returned to design his most amazing Iron Man and War Machine armors to date. Andy Park continued his incredible work on Ant-Man, Hawkeye, Black Widow, and Scarlet Witch; delivered keyframes that will delight any comic-book fan; and created early designs for Black Panther. Rodney Fuentebella found an iconic and tactical look for Crossbones, and painted his signature action-packed frames. Josh Nizzi was responsible for the inspired upgrade to Falcon and Redwing. Josh Herman helped out on most of the characters, but his amazing modeling skills were most important to Iron Man, War Machine, Ant-Man, Spider-Man, and Black Panther. And of course, thanks to Jacob Johnston for being the liaison through which all good information passes, and for writing and assembling the amazing art books.

All the work we do is only a small part of the herculean effort that goes into making these movies. Production Designer Owen Paterson set the scene perfectly. Judianna Makovsky delivered costumes that thrill as much in a wide shot as they do close-up. The characters have never looked better—due in part to Shane, Lindsey, and Chris at Legacy Effects. And all of the digital characters have achieved new heights thanks to Dan Deleeuw, Jen Underdahl, and the multitude of talented VFX artists.

I know I've said I'm lucky a couple times in here. I'm not sure I can say it enough: Working on Captain America, the Winter Soldier, Black Panther, and Spider-Man—all in one movie—makes me the luckiest artist in the film business.

Ryan Meinerding

Directors **Anthony** and **Joe Russo** are perhaps best-known for their work on the critically acclaimed television shows *Arrested Development*, *Community*, and *Happy Endings*. They directed the pilots to all three shows, as well as many of the series' signature episodes. Born a year apart in Cleveland, Ohio, the Russo Brothers used credit cards and student loans to finance their first film *Pieces*, an experimental comedy shot with the help of family and friends. The film screened at both the Slamdance and American Film Institute festivals in 1997, earning Joe a Best Actor award at the latter. The Slamdance screening caught the attention of filmmaker Steven Soderbergh, who along with his producing partner George Clooney, offered to produce the brothers' second film, the crime comedy *Welcome to Collinwood*. Kevin Reilly was rebuilding the FX Network when he first saw *Welcome to Collinwood*, and he asked the pair to direct the pilot for his new flagship comedy, *Lucky*. Among the pilot's fans was Imagine Entertainment co-founder Ron Howard, who, along with writer Mitch Hurwitz, was looking to take the well-worn situation comedy in a new direction. They sought out the Russos to direct the pilot to *Arrested Development*. The brothers shot the show on HD cameras, minimizing the need for complex lighting and crews, and created the distinctive visual style that was so popular with the show's fan base. They won an Emmy for their direction. In 2008, the brothers directed the pilot to *Community*, and in 2009, the pilot to *Happy Endings*. They partnered with Dan Harmon and David Caspe as executive producers and spent the next three years working simultaneously on both shows. Over the last decade, the Russos have directed 12 television pilots, 10 of which have gone to series.

Over the past decade, Producer and Marvel Studios President **Kevin Feige** has played an instrumental role in a string of blockbuster feature films adapted from the pages of Marvel comic books. In his current role, Feige oversees all creative aspects of the company's feature film and home entertainment activities. He is currently producing *Doctor Strange*. His previous producing credits for Marvel include *Iron Man 3*, which became the second-largest box office debut in Hollywood history behind the critically acclaimed *Marvel's The Avengers*, which Kevin also produced along with *Ant-Man*, Marvel's *Avengers: Age of Ultron*, *Guardians of the Galaxy*, *Captain America: The Winter Soldier*, *Thor: The Dark World*, *Thor*, *Captain America: The First Avenger*, *Iron Man 2*, and *Iron Man*.

Executive Producer and Marvel Studios Co-President **Louis D'Esposito** served as Executive Producer on the blockbuster hits *Iron Man*, *Iron Man 2*, *Thor*, *Captain America: The First Avenger*, *Marvel's The Avengers*, *Iron Man 3*, *Thor: The Dark World*, *Captain America: The Winter Soldier*, Marvel's *Avengers: Age of Ultron*, and, most recently, *Ant-Man*. He is currently working on *Doctor Strange*, as well as collaborating with Marvel Studios' President Kevin Feige to build the future Marvel slate. As co-president of the studio and Executive Producer on all Marvel films, D'Esposito balances running the studio to overseeing each film from its development stage to distribution. Beyond his role as co-president, D'Esposito also directs unique projects for the studio, including his one-shot titled *Agent Carter* starring Hayley Atwell, and the short film titled *Item 47*. The project was released as an added feature on *Marvel's The Avengers* Blu-ray disc. D'Esposito began his tenure at Marvel Studios in 2006. Prior to Marvel, D'Esposito's executive producing credits include the 2006 hit film The *Pursuit of Happyness* starring Will Smith, *Zathura: A Space Adventure*, and the 2003 hit *S.W.A.T.* starring Samuel L. Jackson and Colin Farrell.

Executive Producer and Head of Physical Production **Victoria Alonso** is executive producer for Joe and Anthony Russo's *Captain America: Civil War* for Marvel Studios, where she serves as executive vice president of Visual Effects and Post-Production. She executive produced James Gunn's *Guardians of the Galaxy*, Joe and Anthony Russo's *Captain America: The Winter Soldier*, Alan Taylor's *Thor: The Dark World*, Shane Black's *Iron Man 3*, as well as *Marvel's The Avengers* and Marvel's *Avengers: Age of Ultron* for Joss Whedon. She also co-produced Marvel's *Iron Man* and *Iron Man 2* with Director Jon Favreau, Kenneth Branagh's *Thor*, and Joe Johnston's *Captain America: The First Avenger*. Alonso's career began at the nascency of the visual effects industry, when she served as a commercial VFX producer. From there, she VFX-produced numerous feature films, working with such directors as Ridley Scott (*Kingdom of Heaven*), Tim Burton (*Big Fish*), and Andrew Adamson (*Shrek*), to name a few.

Executive Producer **Nate Moore** began his career at Marvel Studios in 2010 working primarily on long lead development and running the Marvel Writers Program. Moore got his start in the film industry working at Columbia Pictures and Exclusive Media working on numerous feature films. An avid Marvel Comics fan, he is excited to help bring to life the expanding world of Captain America.

Co-Producer and Vice President of Physical Production **Mitch Bell** started with Marvel Studios in 2010. He oversaw production and was Associate Producer on *Captain America: The First Avenger*, *Iron Man 3*, and *Captain America: The Winter Soldier*. Bell was executive producer on several Marvel one-shots including *Item 47* and *Agent Carter*. Prior to joining Marvel Studios, Bell was a freelance production supervisor with over 20 years of experience in both features and television. Originally from Fort Collins, Colorado, Bell moved to Los Angeles in the early '90s and started his career as a production assistant at Imagine Films.

Associate Producer **Trinh Tran** is the director of production and development at Marvel Studios and is currently serving as an associate producer for the highly anticipated releases of *Avengers: Infinity War Part I* and *Avengers: Infinity War Part II*. Tran joined Marvel Studios in 2007 as the assistant to the head of post-production, and went on to work for the co-president and head of VFX before she became a creative executive on 2014's *Captain America: The Winter Soldier*.

Production Designer **Owen Paterson** won an Australian Film Institute Award for Best Production Design for Stephan Elliott's *The Adventures of Priscilla, Queen of the Desert*. Most recently, Paterson served as production designer on *Godzilla*, *The Green Hornet*, *Speed Racer*, *V for Vendetta*, and *Gods of Egypt*. His other credits include *Red Planet*, *The Matrix*, *The Matrix Reloaded*, *The Matrix Revolutions*, *Welcome to Woop Woop*, *Race the Sun*, *Minnamurra*, *The Place at the Coast*, and *Traveling North*. Paterson also worked as art director on the Australian features *Bliss* and *The Coolangatta Gold*. His television credits include *Noriega: God's Favorite*, *The Beast*, and the telefilm *The Riddle of the Stinson*.

Director of Photography **Trent Opaloch** started working behind a camera in his early teen years helping his stepfather, a wildlife cameraman, on nature documentaries. After film school Opaloch began his career shooting short films, music videos, and commercials before filming Neill Blomkamp's Oscar-nominated *District 9*. Opaloch's work on *District 9* was nominated for Best Cinematography at the 2010 BAFTA Film Awards as well as the CSC and OFCS awards. In addition to Marvel's *Captain America: The Winter Soldier* and *Captain America: Civil War*, Opaloch's feature film credits include Blomkamp's *Elysium*, starring Matt Damon and Jodie Foster, and *Chappie*, starring Hugh Jackman and Sigourney Weaver.

Costume Designer **Judianna Makovsky** is a three-time Academy Award nominee whose designs for *Seabiscuit*, *Harry Potter and the Sorcerer's Stone*, and *Pleasantville* have been recognized with Oscar nominations as well as being honored by her peers with Costume Designers Guild Awards for the latter two films. She also received a BAFTA nomination for *Harry Potter and the Sorcerer's Stone*. Most recently, Makovsky designed the costumes for *The Hunger Games* and *The Last Airbender*, and the recently completed *Look of Love*. Some of her other credits include *Cirque du Freak*, *X-Men: The Last Stand*, both *National Treasure* films, *The Legend of Bagger Vance*, *Practical Magic*, *Lolita*, *Mr. Brooks*, *A Little Princess*, *The Quick and the Dead*, *The Devil's Advocate*, *White Squall*, *Reversal of Fortune*, and *Great Expectations*. Makovsky has a BFA from The School of the Art Institute of Chicago, and also attended the Goodman School of Drama as well as the MFA program at Yale University School of Drama.

Head of Visual Development **Ryan Meinerding** has only been active as a freelance concept artist and illustrator in the film business since 2005, but his work is already drawing the kind of raves reserved for veterans of the industry. After earning a degree in industrial design from Notre Dame, he transitioned to Hollywood and worked on *Outlander*. Subsequent to *Iron Man*, he worked on *Transformers: Revenge of the Fallen* and illustrated costumes on *Watchmen*. While working on *Iron Man 2*, Meinerding contributed the design for the new Iron Man armor in the comic-book series *Invincible Iron Man*, continuing to cement the strong bonds between Marvel Studios and Marvel Comics. He was part of the Iron Man crew nominated for the 2009 Art Directors Guild Excellence in Production Design Award for Fantasy Films; was one of the main concept designers for *Thor*, and served as Visual Development co-supervisor on *Captain America: The First Avenger* and *Marvel's The Avengers*, and head of Visual Development on *Iron Man 3*, *Captain America: The Winter Soldier*, and *Avengers: Age of Ultron*.

Property Master **Russell Bobbitt's** resume includes all three of Marvel's Iron Man films, *Thor*, and *Captain America: The Winter Soldier*, as well as *Oz: The Great and Powerful*, *The Hangover*, *The Hangover Part II*, and J.J. Abrams' *Star Trek*. Tasked with the design, manufacturing, and acquisition of film props, as well as the establishment of prop continuity from scene to scene, Bobbitt has been developing the physical reality of iconic movies for 30 years. He has twice won Hamilton's prestigious "Behind the Camera" Award for Best Property Master. He has also won two Telly Awards for directing. He resides in Los Angeles with his wife, Tracy, and daughter Jordan.

Visual Effects Supervisor **Dan Deleeuw** grew up in Southern California and started creating effects at an early age. He would spend his summer vacations building miniatures that would be destroyed in spectacular fashion on the 4th of July. After college, Deleeuw started working at Dream Quest Images as the second employee in their digital division. He was digital supervisor on *Crimson Tide*, *The Rock*, and *Reign of Fire*. He branched into character animation, and worked at Rhythm and Hues VFX supervising *Night at the Museum*, which made it to the

Academy VFX Bake-Off. Dan joined the Marvel team when he supervised second unit on *Iron Man 3* and was VFX supervisor for *Captain America: The Winter Soldier*.

Visual Effects Producer **Jen Underdahl's** experience in film and television includes some of Hollywood's most respected films. She has been with Marvel for nearly four years and during that time has served as a VFX executive on the *Marvel's The Avengers*, Visual Effects producer on *Marvel One-Shot: Item 47*, and VFX production manager on *Captain America: The First Avenger*. Prior to working at Marvel she worked freelance on such projects as Gore Verbinski's *Pirates of the Caribbean: At World's End*, the Wachowskis' *Speed Racer*, Chris Columbus' *Percy Jackson and the Lightning Thief*, and Clint Eastwood's WWII duo-film project, *Flags of Our Fathers* and *Letters from Iwo Jima*. Before making the move into digital effects, Jen began her career in the model shop, building practical miniatures and props for film and television. She has been credited on such effects-heavy films as Jon Favreau's *Zathura: A Space Adventure*, Rob Cohen's *Stealth*, and Roland Emmerich's *The Day After Tomorrow*.

Lead Visual Development Concept Illustrator **Andy Park** studied as an Art and Illustration major at both UCLA and Art Center College of Design. His career began as a comic-book artist fulfilling a childhood dream of illustrating titles such as *Tomb Raider*, *Excalibur*, and *Uncanny X-Men* for Marvel, DC, and Image Comics, among others. After a decade in the comic-book industry, he made a career switch and began working as a concept artist in video games and television/film. He was one of the leading artists creating the various worlds and fantastical characters of the award-winning *God of War* franchise for Sony Computer Entertainment of America. Park joined the Visual Development Department at Marvel Studios in 2010 as a visual development concept artist, designing characters and keyframe illustrations for *Marvel's The Avengers*, *Iron Man 3*, *Captain America: The Winter Soldier*, *Thor: The Dark World*, *Guardians of the Galaxy*, *Avengers: Age of Ultron*, *Ant-Man*, *Captain America: Civil War*, and the upcoming *Guardians of the Galaxy Vol. 2* and *Thor: Ragnarok*.

Concept Artist **Rodney Fuentebella** has degrees in design from UCLA and product design from the Art Center College of Design. Born in the Philippines and raised in San Francisco, he has worked on various projects for Electronic Arts, Atari, Rhythm and Hues, DreamWorks Animation, and *WIRED* magazine, as well as various other entertainment and commercial projects. In film, he worked as a concept artist at Rhythm and Hues before joining the Visual Development team at Marvel Studios. Fuentebella has created key-art illustrations and character designs for various projects including *Captain America: The First Avenger*, *Marvel's The Avengers*, *Iron Man 3*, *Captain America: The Winter Soldier*, *Guardians of the Galaxy*, *Avengers: Age of Ultron*, *Ant-Man*, and upcoming Marvel Studios films.

Concept Artist **Josh Nizzi** graduated from the University of Illinois with a degree in Graphic Design. He spent the next nine years working in video games as an art director, concept artist, modeler, and animator on games like *Red Faction 1 & 2*, *The Punisher*, *MechAssault 2*, and *Fracture*. Since then, Nizzi has been an illustrator for feature films such as *Transformers 2, 3, & 4*, *The Amazing Spider-Man*, *Iron Man 3*, *Django Unchained*, and *The Wolverine*. He continues to work on video game projects as well as venturing into toys, comics, and television.

Storyboard Artist **Darrin Denlinger** taught himself to draw by copying Marvel Comics covers all through middle school. After watching *Superman: The Movie* and *Alien* as a teenager, the twin passions of art and cinema sent him on a twisty journey studying film production at SDSU and spending years learning the inner workings of Hollywood in a variety of positions at Universal Studios and Sony Pictures. When dear friend George Huang offered him a chance to do storyboards on his teen comedy *Trojan War*, Darrin had found his calling. Darrin has contributed to a wide variety of films, from *Pirates of the Caribbean* to *Bridesmaids*. Considering his childhood fixation with comic-book covers, Darrin's tenure on Marvel films such as *The Incredible Hulk*, *Thor*, *Captain America: The First Avenger*, *Marvel's The Avengers*, *Iron Man 3*, and *Marvel's Avengers: Age of Ultron* has been a dream come true. Darrin lives in Los Angeles with the love of his life, Mari, and two amazing sons, Aidan and Nate.

Storyboard Artist **Richard Bennett Lamas** is Uruguayan by birth, but moved to New York to start a career in the comic-book field. Over the next ten years, he worked for several companies, including Marvel and Image, before relocating to enroll at the Art Center College of Design in Pasadena. There he studied illustration, and since graduation, he's been working in the motion picture industry. Among some of the films he collaborated on are *AVP*, *Zodiac*, *The Curious Case of Benjamin Button*, *The Social Network*, *Mission: Impossible—Ghost Protocol*, *Oblivion*, and *Star Trek*. More recently he worked on *Tomorrowland*, *Marvel's The Avengers*, and *Captain America: The Winter Soldier*.

Storyboard Artist **Tony Liberatore's** work has spanned the film, television, advertising, and gaming industries since 2001. He now works exclusively on feature films for Marvel Studios, Paramount, Warner Brothers, and Universal Studios. Liberatore is a member of the Local 800, the Art Directors Guild.

Andy Park concept art.

CONTRIBUTOR BIOS 2016

Jackson Sze concept art.

ACKNOWL

Victoria Alonso	Dan Deleeuw	Chris Evans	Scarlett Johansson
Paul Bettany	Darrin Denlinger	Monica Fedrick	Maciej Kuciara
Russell Bobbitt	Erika Denton	Kevin Feige	Richard Bennett Lamas
Chadwick Boseman	Louis D'Esposito	Martin Freeman	Andrew Leung
Don Cheadle	Mariano Diaz	Rodney Fuentebella	Tony Liberatore
Christian Cordella	Robert Downey Jr.	Frank Grillo	Anthony Mackie
Andres Cubillan	John Eaves	Tom Holland	Jerad Marantz

DEMENTS

Judianna Makovsky
Ryan Meinerding
Nate Moore
David Moreau
Josh Nizzi
Marek Okon
Elizabeth Olsen

Brian Overton
Paul Ozzimo
Andy Park
Owen Paterson
Manuel Plank-Jorge
Jacque Porte
Jamie Rama

Jeremy Renner
Paul Rudd
Anthony Russo
Joe Russo
Phil Saunders
Nathan Schroeder
SCPS Unlimited

Sebastian Stan
Jackson Sze
Jen Underdahl
Emily VanCamp

Ryan Meinerding concept art.

ARTIST CREDITS

Ryan Meinerding
Cover
Pages 6-7, 18-21, 78, 82-89, 116-117, 204-205, 214, 242-243, 246-251, 252-265, 270-271

Rodney Fuentebella
Pages 2-5, 16-17, 34-41, 64-65, 118-119, 130-131, 150-151, 174-175, 180-181, 194-195, 214-217, 224, 226-227

Josh Nizzi
Pages 22-25, 159-161, 165, 182-185, 225

Andy Park
Pages 26, 30-31, 80-81, 91-93, 138-139, 152-155, 166-173, 176-177, 186-193, 224, 244-245, 260-263, 267

John Eaves
Pages 27, 52, 96, 132, 155-158, 160, 196-197

Christian Cordella
Pages 28-29, 32-33, 121, 222-223

SCPS Unlimited
Pages 38, 42-43

Mariano Diaz
Pages 44-45, 78-79, 203, 222

Manuel Plank-Jorge
Pages 46-49, 56-59, 76-77, 122, 140-141, 228-229, 231

Marek Okon
Pages 50-55, 60-63, 68-71, 142-143, 232-233

Maciej Kuciara
Pages 56, 72-73, 98-101, 104-109, 206-213, 221, 234-241

Jamie Rama
Pages 66-67

Monica Fedrick
Page 68

Jerad Marantz
Page 90

Phil Saunders
Pages 94-95, 97, 162-165

Darrin Denlinger
Pages 98-99, 102-103, 110-111

Tony Liberatore
Pages 112-115

Nathan Schroeder
Pages 120-123, 230

Paul Ozzimo
Pages 124-129, 132-137, 218-219

Richard Bennett Lamas
Pages 144-149

Jackson Sze
Pages 178-179, 268-269

Andrew Leung
Pages 198-202

Andres Cubillan
Page 203

David Moreau
Page 220